PHOTOBIOGRAPHY

Books by CECIL BEATON

PHOTOBIOGRAPHY · NEW YORK · TIME EXPOSURE (WITH

PETER QUENNELL) · BRITISH PHOTOGRAPHERS · SCRAPBOOK

Cecil Beaton

PHOTOBIOGRAPHY

DOUBLEDAY & COMPANY, INC., GARDEN CITY, NEW YORK, 1951

To EDNA WOOLMAN CHASE *with gratitude and warm affection.*

Acknowledgments

I should like to thank Condé Nast Publications and the British Ministry of Information for their kind permission to use some of the photographs in this book.

C. B.

Contents

Photographs

PHOTOGRAPHS

Chapter 1 FIRST STEPS

ARLY in this century, before the telephone was in general use, when a message could be sent through the post in England for a halfpenny, a flourishing trade provided the public with picture postcards of the musical-comedy actresses of the day. These postcards were sent almost every time an engagement was arranged, or altered, or a friend went away, so that through their likenesses many young women whose talents consisted solely in their photogenic qualities acquired a household fame which their work in the theatre could never have provided. These cards were made of a hardy stiff paper on which the sepia-coloured photograph was printed, then coated with a polished glass finish which produced the illusion that it had come, still wet but immaculately taut, out of a mountain brook. Underneath the picture was the stamp: "This Is a Real Photograph."

The standard of commercial photography at this time was already in its first decline. Far less imagination was shown than in those earlier photographs which depicted for posterity the Victorian era. Vitality and intensity were missing; sitters were now caught in a stylised and somewhat mechanical set of poses against a nebulous background of chalky grey canvas; yet, although the lighting was hard and unsubtle, the sitters often succeeded in looking very pretty.

When I was three years old I used to be allowed to scramble into my mother's large bed and nestle close to her while she sipped an early-morning cup of tea and opened her letters. One morning during this customary treat my eyes fell upon a postcard lying on the pink silk eiderdown in front of me, and the beauty of it caused my heart to leap. The photograph was of Miss Lily Elsie, who had created a legend in the role of the "Merry Widow," and she was here seen with the Greek line of her profile proudly proffered in the fashion of the time; her neck, in its full swanlike glory, was surrounded by an elaborate filigree of diamonds, while her hair was piled in billowing clusters of curls. To make the whole effect more unbearably beautiful, the photograph had been tinted; the cheeks and lips of this divine creature were of a translucent pink that I could never hope to acquire from my box of crayons, and the tulle corsage of her pale yellow dress was spangled with tinsel stardust. My passion for Miss Lily Elsie and my interest in photography were thus engendered at the same moment.

From now on I started to make a collection of picture postcards of my heroine, and the pennies that were given to me as weekly pocket money were no longer spent buying sweets but in enlarging my collection of photographs. Soon I had postcards of Lily Elsie modeling the famous Merry Widow hat, wearing a variety of dazzling evening dresses, and also a Ruritanian costume with gold tinsel loincloth and aigrettes in her curls. I even discovered postcards of my goddess in the intimacy of her own abode near Henley-on-Thames. By degrees my interest spread to other leading ladies of the time; but Lily Elsie was always my unsurpassed, unsurpassable favourite.

At Christmas the most prized item in my stocking, filled with sweets, an orange, a mouth organ, and a Meccano, would be the couple of Rotary or Beagles postcards which showed my idol dreaming over a bunch of florist's roses in a Baker Street studio, or wearing a chiffon dress, on a plough, "leading a country life." My favourite afternoon walks were always to and from the various stationers' in the neighbourhood, where I would turn the revolving stands of glistening postcards; and, having spent half an hour among my beloved hierarchy and the last pennies of my pocket money, I would leave with my purchase clamped tight and hot between thumb and finger, which were thickly encased in a brown woollen glove.

One afternoon the usual timetable was altered; lunch was ordered early, and I was given an extra washing and combing and taken by my mother to be photographed. I was much impressed by the occasion, for the photographer chosen was a Miss Lallie Charles, the very same lady who had taken photographs of a number of my stage goddesses. My mother, in a pink-and-gold evening dress, sat in a tall-backed Cromwellian chair in an unreal world of pale grey canvas; and as I stood by her side in freshly balancoed shoes, taking in my strange surroundings, I was quietly thrilled by the fact that the background stretched underfoot to the glass roof above without division between wall and floor. So overcome was I with emotion and awe that I made a doltish and clumsy sitter, and the placing of one of my podgy hands in the belt of my pale blue suit gave Miss Charles much trouble. But when my mother was presented with a large bunch of roses as a "property" and I discovered that they were false, I suddenly recognised them and, bursting out of

"I was taken by my mother to Lallie Charles's studio and stood awkwardly, overcome by emotion."

my shyness, shouted, "They're the same roses that Lily Elsie held!" At once I grabbed hold of them, but after a certain amount of simpering on the part of Miss Charles, who explained it would not be suitable for a little boy to hold a bunch of roses, I relinquished them with regret.

After a few birthdays my interest in photography began to develop beyond postcards; I had discovered there were other places in which I could find photographs of the much-publicised galaxy of feminine beauty. I now scoured greedily the weekly magazines, the playbills and illustrated programmes, to pore over the details of the pictures taken by Messrs. Foulsham and Banfield, the Stage-Photo Company, Miss Lallie Charles, and her sister Rita Martin, and by degrees I had garnered a large collection of pages carefully extracted from the magazines which were put among my cricket shirts, snake clasp belts, and short trousers in a drawer of my wardrobe. Soon the clothing had to be stored elsewhere, for now the entire drawer was filled with glorious theatrical loot. Photographs, large and small, printed in terra cotta or verdigris green, which was particularly fashionable at this time, photographs cut from everywhere accumulated in such numbers that it was difficult either to open or shut the wardrobe drawers.

The question of the size of the photograph assumed an importance to me, for all the poses seemed equally beautiful, but often my favourites were seen on too small a scale for my liking. "If only that picture had been a full page!" I would moan. Among my nightly prayers was the supplication that in next Tuesday's *Sketch* there might be a double-page photograph of, if not Miss Lily Elsie, then, please, oh Lord, let there be one of Miss Gertie Millar, or, if not of Miss Gertie Millar, please, oh Lord, let there be a simply scrumptious one of Miss Florence Smithson, or, failing her, of Mademoiselle Gaby Deslys!

So absorbed did I become in this somewhat stilted and artificial branch of photography that I cherished even its shortcomings. If an actress were caught in some particularly affected attitude, I was enchanted. Because they appeared behind my favourite's head, the out-of-focus blobs of light, like frog spawn, which misrepresented the sky seen between the leaves of distant trees, had a magic quality for me. I was fascinated by the small stippling marks, which, I soon discovered, were the results of retouching on the negatives, and, once seen, could often be recognised at the waistlines or under the chin of my favourites. To this day the addition of painted eyelashes on the print, a fad of this period, is a convention that delights me. Becoming by this time (I must have been nine years old) completely stage-struck, I followed every activity of the theatre through the pictures which appeared in magazines. I felt a keen perverse enjoyment in scrutinising the photographs of stage scenery. The more blatantly these showed the tricks and artifices of the stage, which would never be obvious to a theatre audience, the greater my pleasure. I would detect every small join in the canvas, or where the artificial roses were nailed onto the painted trellis, and, above all, I loved to peer through a magnifying glass at the tennis netting which hung among the delicate filigree of the tree borders, thus preventing the canvas from hanging back to front or in limp strands.

My father, always a lover of the theatre, was in the habit of making annual business trips to the United States. His return home was, for me, the cause of great excitement, for invariably he brought back from New York with him illustrated play programmes and theatre magazines, which gave me a glimpse of an entirely new hierarchy of stage stars. Having devoured his photographs, I would then bombard him with questions about Hazel Dawn's hair and the exact shade of "The Pink Lady's" hat, and in what details Miss Valli-Valli's "Dollar Princess" differed from our own Lily Elsie's. But on these subjects, try as he did, my father could never be sufficiently explicit. I used to wonder why the Broadway stage scenery looked so real in the photographs, so unlike my ideal stage scenery. I regretted that the chicken wire in the canvas tree trunks and the tennis netting in the trees did not show clearly, as in our Stage-Photo Company's pictures. I did not realise that this was because the Broadway pictures were lit with better photographic equipment, so that they gave almost the same effects seen at the actual stage performances.

One summer day I was taken to the Botanical Gardens in Regent's Park for the Annual Theatrical Charity Garden Party. Here I came face to face with many of the ladies I had known from their picture postcards. My enthusiasm that afternoon at having collected many autographs in my album was already somewhat hysterical, when suddenly I saw displayed before me the Autographed Photograph Stall. Here were the originals of the pictures I knew, printed in apricot-coloured tones on a paper that looked like alabaster with a blue bloom upon the surface. They stimulated me to transports of adolescent ecstasy.

I was now sent, at the age of ten, to a day school, where I should have become absorbed in other interests. But I was profoundly bored by teachers and work, and towards the end of my first term I was discovered drawing in the history class. I received six painful strokes of the ruler across the palm of my right hand. But much worse for me was the fact that my cherished note-book, filled with a hundred drawings—not of Joan of Arc or Queen Elizabeth —but of my Leading Ladies of Musical Comedy, done from memories of my photographic collection, with every detail of their wardrobe most carefully and lovingly reproduced, was confiscated.

One Christmas I was given a Box Brownie Camera, and I tried very hard, but in vain, to photograph my school friends or my parents to look like leading theatrical figures. The results were extremely poor, and large lumps of cotton wool seemed always to be floating in front of my victims. Meanwhile, in the nursery, two younger sisters were growing up. At this time I lived with my family in a rambling house in Hampstead of which the top floor was inhabited by my sisters and their nurse, Alice Collard, known as "Ninnie." Ninnie was an admirable amateur photographer. With her box camera—one size larger than my own—she had always taken snapshots of her various charges and produced remarkably good pictures. Knowing her limitations as a camera operator, she was not adventurous in conquering new fields and never had ambitions to make indoor "time exposures" or "camera portraits." Her clearest results were achieved in the strong sunlight at the seaside, though her most flattering were taken under a cloudy sky in a June garden.

When the lupins and Dorothy Perkins were blooming, and the evening lingered, Ninnie would start her campaigning season. She would click away with confident professionalism. Last thing at night, we used to see her emerge triumphant from the nursery bathroom, carrying in her arms a long strip of freshly developed negative. Next morning, at breakfast time, we were allowed a quick peep at the terra-cotta-coloured sheets of paper already printed by the light of early dawn and now placed for safety in the rice-paper leaves of her Holy Bible. Later that day Ninnie would beam with pride as she produced the finished pictures, now "fixed" with hypo, washed, dried, and pressed. I was extremely envious of her talent. My own pictures seemed never to improve; generally out of focus, often underexposed, there was always a high percentage of failures.

Although I was now about twelve years old and my elder sister was only five years my junior, I was discouraged from visiting too often the upstairs nursery kingdom. No doubt Ninnie had enough to do without onslaughts from other parts of the house, and maybe I taxed her at inconvenient moments by asking advice about how I could emulate her photographic successes, but I knew she could teach me so much. However, sometimes during the winter evenings she allowed me to watch her at work while she printed her favourite summer snapshots on "gaslight printing paper," which gave black-and-white results instead of the richer, Rembrandtesque daylight printing on "sepia velours." While the expert manipulated the wet slithers of paper, washed the prints in basins from the spare-room washstand, or while she pressed the curly paper cylinders with a rubber roller, scrutinised them

My sister Baba in an improvised costume

under a magnifying glass, or transfixed them between the brown pages of canvas-backed albums with a paste which smelled pleasantly of almonds, I would watch with an enthralled admiration.

Sometimes during the summer, as a special treat, I was allowed to watch Ninnie developing her films, and when I bought my own daylight developing tank, in emulation of her, she instructed me how to mix the small packets of acid powders, which smelled of pepper, subsequently pouring the strange brews into various aluminum pots. Then, most mysterious of all rituals, she showed me how to wind the film, wrapped in its black mackintosh belt, through its complicated progress in the hermetically sealed, daylight-proof wooden casket.

Under Ninnie's tuition some of my photographs were successful; but, unlike Ninnie, I was not satisfied to use my box camera for the purpose for which it was intended. My Brownie should have recorded the likenesses of family groups standing in broad sunlight, preferably at the seaside, where the light was said to be so much clearer. When it was put to work emulating the silvery tones of Rita Martin's high-key portraits, the results were sadly inadequate. On my twelfth birthday I was given a present of a No. 3 Folding Pocket Kodak, which produced a postcard-size negative. This was a great technical advance, and, encouraged by the results of the first exterior snapshots, I brought my placid sitters indoors, stood them by the long windows of the dining room, and set the camera stop to "Time Exposure," using the wine cooler as my tripod. Sometimes the camera would slide, during the exposure, on the polished surface of the mahogany, and the results on the negative would be most unexpected; but sometimes I was rewarded by some quite clear, if unflattering, representations of my sisters.

By sheer detection I picked up a few tricks of the theatrical photographic trade, but many mysteries still remained unsolved by me. Never having been to Rita Martin's daylight studio on a roof in Baker Street, I could not imagine how upon this planet that wonderful effect of luminosity, which often enveloped my favourites, could ever have been achieved. But since the indoor time exposures had resulted in so many failures, I would take my studio out of doors and with great enthusiasm pin up some bed linen against a wall in the garden and pose my wretched sisters, holding a bunch of roses, with lowered lids. Alas! My optimism was still unwarranted. The results were disappointing; the table on which I had placed the camera had quivered during the exposure, or I had misjudged the distance of feet between the lens and my subject, who would appear a mere smudge in the foreground, while the background, in all its unsuitable detail of badly creased sheet, tied only too obviously with string and sagging between posts, remained completely sharp, and directly above my sitter's head appeared the small lavatory window of a neighbouring house.

Yet, undaunted, I continued with my ambitious alfresco projects and elaborate arrangements. I carried heavy screens, French drawing-room furniture, and a Dresden bowl of potpourri out into the garden, where my sister Nancy, perhaps now seven or eight years old, would be made to simper in a white wig and crumpled sheet as a most uncomfortable and unconvincing Marie Antoinette. Even to my jejune eyes the results of these "period" pictures were far from satisfactory. Sometimes the negatives were too thin to give any printed result, and I had to content myself by holding the strip of gelatine against some dark object in order to catch a fleeting glimpse of the "positive" image.

Since Rita Martin's studio effects were too elusive, I now embarked upon imitations of the "at home" professional snapshots of actresses that I admired at this time. They were mostly taken by a Miss Compton Collier, who had perfected a technique of beautifying her sitters in a flat lighting as they sat by an ornamental wellhead or lingered on the crazy paving of their Thames Valley gardens. Miss Collier's snapshots proved much more rewarding goals, and soon my "daylight developing tank" was working overtime, the basins in the washrooms were filled with sepia prints, and the window ledges ornamented with printing frames filled with increasingly successful results. I would take my sisters out, with baskets of tea, black-currant sandwiches, and theatrical properties, into neighbouring woods or gardens to pose as such oddly assorted personalities as Gina Palerme, Laurette Taylor, Ida Adams, or Gladys Cooper. For several weeks I became enamoured of Pavlova, and my sister Nancy would be made to pose with a chiffon scarf draped over her head, looking as much as possible like the pictures I had seen of the great dancer taken in her Ivy House facing Hampstead Heath. My enthusiasm blinded me to the fact that my prima ballerina was a scrawny schoolgirl wearing thick brown socks and heavy shoes.

The summer holidays was still the most productive season of my photographic year. My father considered that a holiday, above everything, must be bracing; so each August we were taken to combat the rigours of a Norfolk summer. Here on the cobblestones of the seashore at Sheringham or Cromer, Ninnie would continue her photographic campaign, but I would inveigle my sisters to the neighbouring woods and the cornfields where, in improvised dresses made of paper and tulle, I would photograph them as medieval princesses or as very respectable nymphs and bacchantes. I was also extremely taken by bridal photographs, and my sisters, in imitation of the photographs of Audrey James or Paula Gellibrand which I had admired in the society

Nuns and brides in the nursery. The costumes comprised towels, sheets, handkerchiefs, and safety pins.

magazines, were often posed as improvised brides in bath towels and syringa. The current fashions, when dresses hung like sacks from a square neck with a loose waistband around the hips, were extremely easy to imitate, and a large bath towel and two safety pins were all that was needed to make an excellent imitation of a wedding dress from Worth or Reville and Rossiter. Worn with the customary brow-level bandeau or headache band of flowers threaded through a tape, the general effect they produced was most convincing.

One sunny afternoon, when we were staying in a horrid little villa at Sheringham, I planned an elaborate wedding for my photographic purposes. Nancy, as a bride in bath towels and marguerites (syringa no longer being in season) and wearing a borrowed pair of my mother's pink brocade high-heeled shoes, attended by her sister Baba in gym shoes, a white party dress, and a bandeau of marguerites, and by some neighbour's child, also dressed more or less in this somewhat bizarre manner, was driven around the block of red brick villas to arrive back beneath a shower of confetti inside the privet hedge surrounding the small property in which we were temporarily quartered. My Kodak was snapping away overtime and I could hardly turn the crank fast enough for the next exposure. Unfortunately the imitation news pictures were somewhat disappointing—the bride appeared like ectoplasm in a spiritualist's photograph. The formal wedding groups, however, thanks to a great deal of retouching on the negatives, were much more satisfactory.

It was the failure to get any result from an attempt to photograph Queen Alexandra at Sandringham that finally taught me that the lens of my camera was too weak to take instantaneous photographs on a cloudy day. My family and I had motored from our holiday quarters in Sheringham to a Sandringham Rose Show, and I shall always have a vivid recollection of this frail, exquisite old lady in black jet, with silhouette as simplified as that of a Minoan sculpture, as she walked among us on the lawns. Her complexion was like pink-and-white icing sugar, and the perfect oval of her face and head turned and bowed from side to side on a neck so slender that it was like a flower too heavy for its stalk. My disappointment on discovering that I had missed this one opportunity and had not caught on my negative even a pale ghostly image stimulated me forthwith to purchase a tripod for my camera in order to take time exposures out of doors. I now gave such lengthy exposures that the negatives were almost too opaque to be printed, a fault, incidentally, which has been apparent in my work ever since, for even today I am apt to give a longer exposure than my meter tells me I need.

On one occasion, after I had written successfully to get permission to photograph with a tripod in a public garden in Hampstead, and after I had made many elaborate preparations, my sisters and I went off to take sensational pictures in the Pavlova manner. I would spend as long as half an hour in arranging the picture before making each new exposure, but my sisters posed to the best of their ability, the day was bright, the herbaceous borders were at their peak, and at the end of the afternoon I felt certain I had produced a dozen masterpieces of the photographic art.

On my return home I went immediately to my bathroom to start the job of developing. I was never adept at the technical part of the business, and on this occasion, in my over-anxiety, I made some fatal error, for when three quarters of an hour later I opened the daylight developing tank and unrolled the porpoise-like belt, it was to find that only small patches of the gelatine had been touched by the acids and that the film of twelve valuable exposures was therefore ruined. My despondency, however, did not last long. And now that my camera was safely secured to a stand, why should I not come indoors once more and try to produce time exposures?

One morning I embarked upon taking a particularly elaborate picture. My sister Baba, then aged about seven, with a tight gold ribbon bound low around her brow, was almost lost in a voluminous dark green opera coat trimmed with ermine that I had filched from my mother's cupboards. In order to raise her to adult height she had to stand on a footstool by a specially draped sofa, with the velvet coat worn as a cloak, in order to hide gym shoes and footstool. I placed an art pot so; a brass tray was hung on the nursery wall. The completion of all these arrangements took quite a considerable time; my sister soon found the cloak of an almost unendurable weight, and it kept slipping off her shoulders and falling to the floor to reveal a pathetic-looking little waif as scraggy as an ortolan.

I was too involved with the intricacies of the camera and tripod to be conscious of the fact that, after standing still for half an hour, tears started to well into the painted eyes of my sister and to course down her cheeks. When at last I gave a final glance at her before making the time exposure, a sorry sight presented itself; the painted face had become a shining pulp; the coat sagged sadly to reveal half a school dress and one gym shoe. I expostulated violently. Surely it was not too much to ask my sister to keep still while I had so many things to attend to! Whereupon Ninnie hustled into the room and put an end to the proceedings; for, she said, it was no use upsetting the child, and the Irish stew was ready.

After several months of experiment I felt that, with luck and Ninnie's guidance, I could produce a postcard-size snapshot which, when mounted upon brown cardboard, with my signature scrawled in a corner, looked almost professional. At this time photography, in my mind, was a mixture of brown cardboard albums, hypo, sepia prints floating in washhand basins or drying on

My sister Nancy. These are early attempts at portraiture. Note lack of composition and the leaking bellows of the camera.

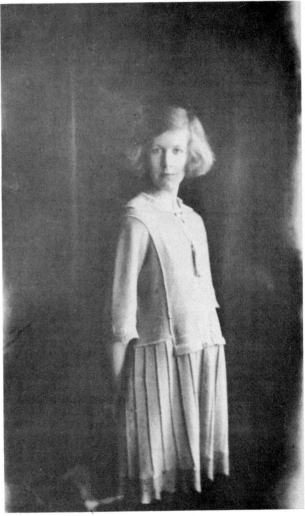

bath towels, the sudden arrival on trays of nursery lunches of fish and tapioca pudding, and salt; the salt was an important element since it was used both for the meals and for giving a darker, cooler tone to the terra-cotta prints.

During the winter the exposures I had to give to make my indoor photographs were of such length that my sisters were seldom able to remain still enough. I longed to possess artificial lights, but the nearest I came to this goal was when I acquired a packet of flashlight powders. Now, from time to time, the house was rocked with sudden explosions, subsequently to become filled with peppery smoke. The results of these flashes were far from satisfactory; the faces of my sisters could be seen faintly emerging from blackness with a look of terror in their eyes. After this I learned that by burning magnesium wire it was possible to obtain a light bright enough in which to take photographs. These results were somewhat more successful, but often the strips of wire took several seconds to catch alight, yet, once aflame and burning with their actinic brilliance, there was no means of blowing them out, so that almost every exposure resulted, since no improvised holder proved adequate, in yelps of pain as my fingers were being badly burned and my fingernails charred.

On my postcard-size negatives I now did a great deal of improvised retouching. Often with blunt pocketknives and clogged jay nibs I made a horrid mess, but I found that by employing all sorts of trickery when contact-printing I was able to get remarkably satisfactory soft-focus effects with my negatives. Once it came to enlarging them, I was up against a very much more difficult proposition, for when my efforts at retouching were enlarged the results suggested that my sitters were in a serious condition of putrefaction. In spite of the many new gadgets and ingenious additions to my photographic paraphernalia, my indoor photographs continued to be unreliable. Nevertheless, I was undaunted.

I was sent to Harrow School where, on my window sill, a couple of printing frames were invariably to be seen by those passing in the High Street. Although a few of my housemates were enthusiastic amateur photographers and during the hours of leisure in the evenings produced excellent enlargements of their holiday snapshots, their approach to the subject was so highly technical and their aims so different from mine that, instead of learning from them, I left them to their strong-smelling brews in aluminum trays from which a portrait of a railway train or a grouse moor would emerge, and carried on my own picture making independently and secretively. Some of my school fellows were as scornful of my somewhat theatrical and affected-looking pictures as I was of their railway trains.

Harrow School did not provide me with many good opportunities for photography, and in desperation a friend and I took to some neighbouring woods, with an assortment of many extraordinary fancy-dress garments, where we photographed one another in the most artistic manner possible. But activities such as these had to be furtive and came to an abrupt end one early morning.

My friend and I decided we would risk taking pictures in our house-master's garden below his windows before he or any of the household was awake. With the earliest rays of sunlight we were out among the shrubberies, taking turns photographing each other in classical poses; we were confident that for another hour or so we would be safe from detection.

Unfortunately we had miscalculated. Perhaps a shaft of brilliant sunlight had penetrated through the drawn curtains of Major and Mrs. Freeborn's bedroom and had awakened Mrs. Freeborn earlier than usual. When she drew back the curtains and looked down into the garden below, she could not quite believe her eyes. Two half-naked figures in Greco-Roman draperies were bounding about her rockery or were posturing like statues under her trees. She called Major Freeborn to her side. The two of them looked on in amazement. By degrees other faces appeared at other windows. I looked up to find, with horror, that we had a large but silent audience which, as soon as we started to bolt for safety, greeted us with hoots, catcalls, and cries of derision.

Any further attempts at photography had to be postponed until the holidays, when by chance I read of a small inexpensive instrument which could be attached to the trigger of any camera to make a delayed-action exposure. The "Automatic Self-Portrait Release," in my possession, worked beautifully, and whenever the mood was upon me, and if my mother was not available for photography, or my sisters were busy with their homework, I could now photograph myself. By placing looking glasses in front of the camera, I discovered the effects of my own physiognomy when the lights were placed at different vantage points. After pressing the release lever, a loud bee-buzz continued for about ten seconds, until the lens clicked for the exposure. It was a cold-blooded and slightly sinister procedure, and I would become acutely embarrassed if ever caught in the act of self-photography. By the time I was eighteen I had learned much about the effects of lights placed at given positions on my own face, and this experience has been useful when photographing the features of others.

Apart from watching Ninnie at work, I never had any lessons in photography. My training in learning how to take, develop, enlarge, retouch, and mount photographs was solely by experiment. The instructions in a technical book on photography, halfheartedly carried out by me, would always produce

My sisters Nancy and Baba in a Victorian background rigged up on a four-poster bed

disastrous results; I was obliged to acquire my own technique. My lack of scientific ability, however, was outweighed by my enthusiasm, which, allied to a certain amount of ingenuity, led me to create in an ordinary London house, without artificial light, many of the trick effects of lighting that leading fashionable photographers employed in elaborately equipped studios. If a certain effect could not be arrived at in the drawing room, then I would take my sitter upstairs to stand against a wall in an attic where I knew that the effect I desired could be created by the light from a small window. Or again, in the loft by the water cistern, there was a skylight which gave me the lighting effect employed by Raeburn, Lawrence, or the other classical English portrait painters.

Having developed a mania for early Victorian decoration and collected shell flowers under glass domes, beadwork chairs, and mother-of-pearl tables, I always introduced them into the elaborate snapshots which I took in imitation of the work of Octavius Hill and other pioneers of photography. One morning I decided that my four-poster bed, which was hung, quite unsuitably, with a theatrical material of scarlet sateen stamped with a medieval design in gold paint, would form a good frame for a Victorian group picture. I set to work to construct an elaborate scene. On the bed itself I laid a large table top to use as a rickety flooring. Upon this were placed Victorian chairs and tables, with the inevitable glass dome of flowers; but the flooring did not reach far enough, so the ironing board was added to give stability to a chair leg.

My sisters, immediately upon their return for luncheon from their day school, were obliged to put on crinolines and have their faces heavily painted. Since I had the Patent Self-Portrait Release I was also to participate in this group and was already dressed with side whiskers, long frock coat, and high cravat. Everything was prepared; the camera was quite steady on the rickety tripod with the Self-Portrait Release all set to go. My sisters had been lifted into their positions without disaster; all that remained was for me to set in motion the bee-buzzing contraption, then deftly mount the bed to take my place in the group. This sounds simple, but in fact, as soon as the automatic release had been freed, panic spread among us. One sister would squeak that a heavy lock of hair had fallen over half her face, the other that her shawl had refused to remain in position and was revealing her poorly improvised bodice. Yet, once it had been set in motion, nothing would stay the automatic release which continued its bee-buzzing with sinister relentlessness. In my dash from camera to bed-top stage I would trip over a leg of the tripod, causing the camera to crash to the floor. Camera scrutinised, mended, and put in place again on its tripod, another attempt would be made. This time as I mounted the stage, the entire bed would lurch like a ship in a hurricane, and the lens would click before we had time to rearrange ourselves. Once again we would try.

With experience I became quicker at ascending the stage, but then, during the sudden lull, awaiting the inevitable buzz, I became convulsed with amusement and, incapable of keeping still, spluttered with inane laughter. In the middle of each picture I would start to tremble, then snort, and infect my sisters with amusement so that they would join me in a hopeless jellied shaking. Finally, outside the locked door, someone shouted that luncheon was ready. Yet, when these results appeared, my sisters pronounced them quite successful, for here at last, they said, they were seen, not looking either angry or bored, while I had been unable to apply my usual set photographic face.

By painful stages I began to master a homemade technique of photography. The goal at which I still aimed was to make successful imitations of the camera portraits in the windows of the seaside photographer or the most straightforward commercial pictures of stage stars. One day, when looking through the photographs in American magazines, I discovered in *Vogue* the work of Baron de Meyer, who, with his camera, took pictures that appeared to be nearer to silver points or engravings than to photography as I had hitherto known it. Even the texture of these photographs, so soft and yet so precisely defined, was unlike anything I had seen before. De Meyer's subjects were elevated to an unreal plane of elegance and perfection and restored to their pristine beauty as though the dew were still upon them. One lady, I remember, was caught posing like a Dresden figure against some scintillating firework display, and her face was bathed in an aura of incandescence that surely came from the moon itself.

A new silvery world was opened to me. De Meyer's work was the epitome of artificiality and luxury and became the ideal towards which I must strive. But how could I, with my No. 3A Kodak and crude lighting equipment, ever attempt to tread this dazzling but difficult path? I had set myself an almost impossible task. Yet so great was my enthusiasm for the master's photographs that I became dissatisfied with the work of all other photographers. I was determined to bring a little of this silvery magic into my attempts. I had already found it difficult enough to obtain sufficient general light for the exposures on my Kodak, but now I must photograph my subjects with such a welter of radiance enveloping them from behind that their transparent skirts were bathed in a glorious halo, their hair an aureole of spiders' skeins, their faces seen in its becoming reflections.

My first attempts at imitating De Meyer were sadly childish. Nonetheless,

My sisters Nancy and Baba. An early photograph.

even my failures had more merit than my earlier snapshots, and I could not have fallen under a more helpful influence. By degrees, however, I achieved an effect of artificial light by reflecting a small patch of sunlight from one window, back and forth, from sometimes as many as six dressing-table mirrors. Thus I was able at least to illuminate the hair around the nape of my sitter's head, and a cheval glass played an important role in relaying the sun onto the crook of my sitter's arm as she sat, inevitably, with one hand on her hip.

I trick-printed my negatives, and when enlarging my pictures I shaded the sitter's hair during the exposure with pieces of cotton wool attached to hat-pins, so that it became blond and silken. The lenses of my enlarger were altered during the exposures, and I became master of all varieties of soft-focus texture which showed, miraculously enough, a richness of tone with a clarity of detail utterly unlike the hard contact prints a shop would have supplied from my negatives. To enlarge one very dense negative took some-times as long as three quarters of an hour; but now and then the print would emerge with just the sentimental effect that I desired.

I believe the work of De Meyer has never been estimated as highly as it warrants. In his last years it was treated with a supercilious scorn, then finally ignored. He died unnoticed and penniless in Hollywood, where his work was unknown, yet where every day in the studios the "Still" cameramen, as well as the film operators, were employing many of the tricks of technique that De Meyer had invented. In the realms of fashion photography he ex-erted greater influence than any other photographer; and in any issue of *Vogue* or *Harper's Bazaar* during the past twenty years it is easy to point out a number of pictures which are derived directly from him. The ladies with hips thrust forwards and arms posed as in a frieze, one foot pointed towards the camera, the upturned head, the general tilt backwards of the body were all part of De Meyer's stock in trade.

To this day, when I encounter some woman difficult to photograph in any other way, I resort to De Meyer's expedient of photographing her with *"profil presque perdu,"* almost silhouetted against a bright light; and it is he who too often persuaded me, in almost every studio picture I take, to give a dazzle to the hair by placing a brilliant lamp above the sitter's head.

My family now moved to Number 3, Hyde Park Street, a large and austere house. Having taken a hand in decorating it to look slightly more theatrical than my parents would have liked, I proceeded to bring my photo-graphic activities into every room. My sisters continued to show compassion to me in my mania and at all times of day and night were called upon to drape themselves in sheets and dustcloths. Carpets were spotted with acids, and I would burst into the dining room in the middle of a family dinner party to show my latest prints dripping onto a towel, the dining table, or the clothes of all to whom they were shown. My mother endured with good grace the havoc created in her well-organised house.

Baba, now ten years old, not only posed with monumental patience, but used to help me after dinner during the long tedious sessions of developing and printing my negatives. She was paid sixpence an hour for her aid, but I knew that often she gave me her support more out of pity than from any love of gain. With a lock of hair almost falling into the tray of acid, she would pore over the various mixtures, watching while an image appeared on a blank piece of paper, till, after a series of yawns, at last she could no longer bear the ordeal and would retire to bed, leaving me to my own resources for the remainder of the night.

Long after the rest of the household was asleep I would work by the light of an electric bulb, swathed in an old red shirt, awaiting the appearance of one perfect print. As the night advanced and the skies turned from black to grey, the red shirt would become singed and the air of the room thickened with the smell of scorching cloth. Eventually, racked with weariness and headache, I was forced to give up. I would cross the dark landing to the bathroom, switch on the light, and discover that the prints floating in the cold water, even in this artificial light, seemed to have an ominously yellow tinge. Sure enough, next day, in the clear blue light of morning, I would find my fears well founded; because I had failed to mix the expensive powders in exactly the right proportions, a large batch of romantic and atmospheric enlargements on valuable enlarging paper had turned during the night to daffodil yellow or marigold orange.

For some time to come my sitters consisted of my immediate family, and it was often difficult to force them to pose. My mother strongly objected, in the middle of a busy morning, to being made to put on a full evening dress. Sometimes she lingered and would come downstairs so late that by the time I was ready to click the camera at her (and I took a great deal of time in arranging each pose) my ingenious arrangements, which looked like an illustration by W. Heath Robinson with looking glasses reflecting the sun, would have been cancelled out by the passage of a cloud or the movement of the sun. Before a new arrangement could be completed, luncheon or tea seemed always to be ready; and as I look back on those pioneer days I marvel at my persistence and at the patience of my family.

At this period my ambition was to have my photographs shown at the Royal Photographic Society's salon, and I spent much time concocting pictures which I intended should make a stir when exhibited at the society's galleries situated off the Haymarket. My money was squandered on tinsel draperies for properties and backgrounds, and a great deal of time was devoted to concocting appropriate titles. The titles most popular in photographic circles at the moment were "Spanish Lady," "Phyllis with Cigarette," "An Old Salt," or "O Sole Mio." I conceived that "Barbara in Gold" would be a suitable title for a picture of my younger sister, and set about buying some brilliant tinsel from Burnet's in Covent Garden.

This shop was, to me, for many years an Aladdin's cave, and I never ceased to marvel at the treasures of fish-scale tissues, the pseudo-Florentine brocades, the tinsel nets, the imitation leopard skin and varieties of "animal baize," and, above all, the highly glazed mackintosh called "American cloth." This material, which I used in many of my earliest photographs, was later employed in so many tawdry theatrical productions that it became just as banal as it had once seemed startlingly original. Inevitably I frequented the counter supervised by Mr. Latchford, who took as much trouble to gratify my wishes when I was able to afford only one and a half yards of stamped sateen as afterwards when I could give him important orders for my theatrical or film work.

"Barbara in Gold" was rejected by the salon's hanging committee; but it was largely due to Mr. Latchford that I was able to produce other photographs which at length were shown at the London Salon. The Private View Day was always a great occasion for pride, curiosity, and envy.

I spent much energy in sending my photographs to the weekly society magazines; but the occasions when a picture of my sisters, disguised as grownups in imitation Renaissance brocades, was accepted for publication were necessarily infrequent, and I became hardened to receiving the printed slip with "the editor's thanks and regrets." I felt uncomfortable at continually sending photographs of my own sisters to the magazines; but, since they were my only sitters, I had no choice and would post them from various addresses under different assumed names. There was great excitement when a rather baffled aunt telephoned to say she had received at her address a note informing her that Liadov's portrait of Miss Nancy Beaton had been accepted for publication in a forthcoming issue of *Britannia & Eve*.

Whenever a picture of mine was published there was great jollification throughout the entire household. Sometimes I was too impatient to await the delivery at the house of the weekly magazines, and on Tuesday at midday hour I would repair to my local news agent to await the arrival of the new *Sketches* and *Tatlers*. My sisters recently reminded me of a day when they were returning from school for lunch and I rushed up the street to welcome them with wild gesticulations and the news that "It's in! It's in, and it's a full page!"

*My mother in stencilled sateen, a victim of my medieval period.
Note crude retouching.*

PHOTOBIOGRAPHY

Some extracts from the diary I kept during the early nineteen-twenties may help to give an impression of my early experiences as a photographer:

Instead of going to see Pavlova, I spent the evening enlarging. I enlarged quite a lot of that perfect Madonna one of Mama, but I did not get a perfect print. I was rather annoyed. I went on enlarging and it got so late and enlarging takes such a time. At about twelve o'clock a terrible thing happened. I was holding the standard lamp to look at a print in the acid when the wire knocked a huge china basin full of acid over me and the carpet and the basin smashed into a thousand bits. I got into a panic. I tidied the room as best I could and swamped the floor and carpet with water, and I scrubbed and swabbed with a nail brush. I put my trousers (luckily old flannel ones) in a basin of water. I was exhausted and came downstairs and ate some plums. In the evening post was one of my photographs returned from the *Bystander* with quite a friendly letter.

Monday, August 9th

The sun came out and I was making the best of my printing time. I became very excited over a new method of printing I've invented which gives the most perfect results. I half-print a photograph through a thickness of glass, and it makes the print all blurred; then for the other half of its printing time I print it sharp on the blurred image so that the effect is marvellously soft as well as detailed. In this way all those negatives can be made into beautiful prints, and, what's more, I shall do the same with the enlarger when it arrives.

I arranged my bedroom for some photographs—photographs of my sister draped in tissue to be called "Barbara in Gold," which I'd been thinking about such a lot when I was ill. Today I felt strong enough, and Baba came up and was nearly naked in five minutes, and then I wrapped this gold stuff round her. She looked quite perfect—like a bit of ancient Venice. I got her arms twisted tightly and I was rather agitated as I was taking the photographs with Daddy's old camera which I had not used before. I took four of Baba, mostly sitting with a book and looking languid or majestic, but I took one other reading our family Bible, side-face and looking marvellous—thin and lithe. I was very excited and hot; Baba rushed downstairs.

I stopped at Tattersall's, a wallpaper shop of the Edgware Road, where an old man was most attentive and tried very hard to get me some paper that I want for photographic backgrounds. I want something terribly rough that will photograph like Hugh Cecil's backgrounds. Gold, of course, is what I want; but I haven't the money for it. The old man told me to go to Scott's in Berners Street, and here I got just what I wanted; I was very thrilled. I looked at lots of things—quite useless; then the bright young man told me he had a small amount of real old Japanese paper which had gone bad with being kept in a damp place. It was marvellous; gold and old and mottled, which was just what I wanted. I took away 25/—worth for 5/—! and was very pleased with myself. I stuck it up in my room and gloated with pleasure. I could not wait to take pictures there and then, but Mummie was out to tea; in any case, we had had a bit of a row this morning, as Mummie wouldn't let me take her photograph once more. It's really rather awful; I get such good ideas, and for weeks and weeks on end I'm not allowed to take a photograph of Mummie, and when I do it's so rushed that there's no possible hope for a successful and artistic picture.

I went to the nursery and found Nancy and Baba returned from their swimming lessons. I told them about my new background and how delighted I was and asked Nancy to let me take her, as I wanted to finish a film and develop it immediately; but Nancy was adamant in her refusal. I was livid. I called her a little beast. She was all white with wet hair and mulish, and so Baba, after much persuasion, came up and was rolled into her gold again. She looked lovely, and I put the gold on in a better way. The two pictures were taken and Baba looked perfect and kept more still than usual.

I rushed downstairs; large basins—water—ice—acids. It's all rather a strain developing in this hot weather, but still I simply couldn't wait. Baba came in the darkroom and was surprised how much lighter it became after we'd been in it a little time. I raised the film first one side, then another; up, down, up, down, like a seesaw, and the red light was so dim that we couldn't see anything on the film for ages. At last I saw. Damn, damn, damn, damn! The wretched view finder (not, not my fault!) was in the wrong place for the lens, and Baba's head was cut off in most of the photographs. I was livid! That was obviously what was wrong, and besides the view finder being too high for the lens, it was also too much to the left. I was livid. I took the camera to Daddy and we found that we could move the view finder to suit the camera, but I was quite livid. Otherwise the photographs looked perfect—all soft, and yet detailed, and the gold looking marvellously golden and Baba looked superb. After dinner I came up to my room and tried once more some gaslight printing. Every damned thing was done too little. I wasted sheets and sheets of paper, and have only about one success out of two packets. I was very tired but went on getting more and more exasperated, and when at last I went to bed, I was almost too tired to sleep. Next day, directly after lunch, Baba once more kindly permitted me to take her photographs in gold again. She posed marvellously—body all one-sided and going one way, and her head all one-sided going the other way, and she put on a marvellous expression—very pitiful and perfect; but Mummie kept shouting for her to come down and go out.

September 6th

After breakfast I got my film and started to print it. As negatives, nothing could be more perfect—so contrasting. This morning was dim and grey, but the things didn't take long to print on the windowsill. The ones of Mummie are quite good, but very bad lines and shadows on the face. They'll need a lot of very careful and clever retouching. I went out to buy a retouching outfit, but I might as well have not wasted my money, for the little box is full of rubbish, and I can touch up just as well without the special things. I've used paint and ordinary pencils before, but in the box there is some special kind of paint, and some medium which I hate; it makes the negatives so sticky.

I came back here and started the touching up. I worked most carefully. My eyes ached, but that didn't matter. I spent the afternoon touching up. I finished one good one of Mummie; also one that is not so good. I became very weary, and my back ached; also my eyes, and my head rather. I began to feel very ill. My eyes ached, my head ached, and I decided to go to bed.

Chapter 2 *JEJUNE ENTHUSIASMS AND EXCITEMENTS*

W H E N in 1922 I arrived at Cambridge I set about becoming a rabid aesthete with a scarlet tie, gauntlet gloves, and hair grown to a flowing length. I took a passionate interest in the Italian Renaissance, Diaghilev's Russian ballet, and, of course, in the theatre and in photography. By this time I had completely mastered the limitations of the folding snapshot camera and knew that, technically at any rate, each roll of film would produce clear, sharp, and well-exposed negatives.

Now, for the first time, I acquired a studio. For a half crown a week I rented a strange loft above an electrician's shop in a lane running at the side of the Union Club. This Dickensian attic was reached by a perilous ascent up some ladder-like stairs from the store, which was filled with accumulator jars, electrical wires, and strange-looking apparatus. The floor boards of my eyrie were uneven and incomplete, so that one could look down upon the incomprehensible activities of the shop below. The walls were of whitewashed brick, which made splendid backgrounds, and at most unexpected angles in wall and roof there were a number of windows which provided almost every conceivable form of natural lighting effect.

Although I had originally intended to devote myself to painting and had equipped myself with elaborate easels and even a long medieval robe to be used as an overall, it was in photographic experimenting that I spent many an afternoon here. To this curious room I invited the more artistic of the dons' wives with their Spanish shawls and daring Eton crops; but at the outset my sittings had to be somewhat surreptitious, as the dons had not made up their minds yet if photography was or was not an art. Some of the more tractable undergraduates came wearing their turtle-neck sweaters or hunting clothes to sit on a trestle table or in a theatrical throne chair. My properties consisted of a dusty model frigate which I had bought from a local antiquary, and an accumulator jar from the shop below which I filled with branches of magnolia leaves.

Towards the end of the term the actors appearing in the Amateur Dramatic Club productions, or those of the Marlowe Society, would be inveigled to pose in their stage costumes. I had recently acquired a passion for Botticelli and Filippo Lippi; and when I photographed Steven Runciman wearing his thick black hair in a fringe, with a budgereegah poised on his ringed finger, looking obliquely into the camera in the manner of the Italian primitives, I knew I had not lived in vain.

Having tried almost every sort of experiment in natural illumination, I now asked the electrician in the shop below if he could produce a sufficiently high-powered lamp for photographic purposes. A few days later he was able to provide a rudimentary version of the lamp I wanted; at a shout from me a switch was turned on in the shop below, and my loft was bathed in a dazzling glow of artificial brilliance to which even my weak-lensed snapshot camera, intended for use in strong daylight, reacted quite favourably. Now, at last, with one big lamp I could surely approximate those effects of back-lighting which had been so magically invented by Baron de Meyer. When I placed this huge bulb behind my sitter's head, the Spanish shawls of the dons' wives would become spiders' webs of filigree threads and the dusty wooden frigate which they proffered so self-consciously became a vessel of spun glass.

Among my contemporaries whom I photographed was George Rylands of Kings College. He showed great enthusiasm for my work and brought it to the attention of Dorothy Todd, who then reigned over certain aesthetic circles in London as the high-brow editress of *Vogue* magazine. During Miss Todd's editorship *Vogue* made many discoveries in the fields of art and literature and published the work of a remarkable collection of younger writers, poets, and painters, often for the first time. Even today these quarter-of-a-century-old issues of *Vogue* are of extraordinary interest, and not merely as nostalgic period pieces. Many of the literary "features" are as compelling as when they first appeared.

At Cambridge each issue of *Vogue* was received as an event of importance; and when one day Miss Todd wrote to me from her Mount Olympus home in Bloomsbury inviting me to photograph some of the poets and writers whom she had unearthed in the neighbourhood of the university city, I felt I was on the road to fame. My first photograph published in *Vogue* was of the "Duchess of Malfi," with clasped hands and wrapt expression, gazing through a haze of incandescent light. The effect was exceedingly romantic. In actual fact, the Duchess of Malfi was George Rylands in the Marlowe Society's production of Webster's play, posing in coif and draperies outside

Lady Diana Cooper. One of my first photos taken with an 8 x 10 camera. The beauty of the subject overcame the crude lighting.

Lady Oxford and Asquith in a "futuristic" background. 1927.

the gentlemen's lavatory in the A.D.C. theatre vestibule. Apart from the honour and glory reflected upon me by the words "Photograph by Cecil Beaton" in minute lettering at the bottom right-hand corner of the picture, I was paid the welcome sum of thirty shillings.

Most of my Cambridge time was spent in rehearsing plays produced by the Marlowe Society or the A.D.C., in which I acted, designed the sets and costumes, and painted the scenery. Whenever possible I motored to London to see the latest plays, or picture and sculpture exhibitions, and many whole days were spent taking photographs. It was an extremely happy time. I was not burdened by responsibilities, and I managed somehow to avoid all lectures or work of any kind. It is not surprising that after three years I left Cambridge without a degree.

I was now twenty years old, and I had no ideas as to the future. When I was at Harrow School I had rather vaguely wished to become a Royal Academician and dedicate myself to portrait painting in an oak-panelled studio, with suits of armour in dark corners and an old piece of brocade negligently thrown over the minstrel's gallery. I would paint fashionable portraits for vast fees, and "varnishing" day would be a great social event. But now "Art" had a different connotation for me. I could not imagine Picasso, Marie Laurencin, or even Bakst, by whom I was now influenced, entertaining on "varnishing" day, and visions of the Luke Fildes, de Laszlo, Frank Dicksee life vanished from my mind.

Although I had a secret longing to become an actor, I felt diffident about taking the necessary first steps. I made rather tentative efforts—without success—to design scenery and costumes for the London stage; but most of my energy—and any spare cash I could find—was spent on taking photographs. Back in London, in my parents' house in Hyde Park Street, the entire drawing room must necessarily be turned upside down each time a sitting was embarked upon. Invariably each session lasted much longer than had been intended, and there was a breathless scramble to tidy up before the arrival of my mother's guests.

At this period our butler, or family factotum, named Loins, decided that, although the housemaids were responsible for clearing up the mess, the disturbance caused in the household by my photography was too difficult to contend with and gave in his notice. Loins was succeeded by Manley, a white-faced little man with jet-black hair who looked like a tragic waxwork figure but whose innate gaiety and high spirits belied the pathos in his eyes. Manley enjoyed the eccentricities of our family and was appreciative of the enthusiasms and interests of each member of the household. He competed tactfully with all our various telephone messages and managed to achieve more in a day than three men together. Although it meant added work for him, he enjoyed helping me at the photographic sessions. He would carry back and forth, always with the same good humour, in and out of the conservatory, the heavy screen pasted with tinsel paper which I now invariably used for my backgrounds, and, whenever the light failed, always came to my rescue in changing the fuses. He would then climb a ladder and hold a lamp over my sister's hair, and during the long exposure would show his amusement by snorting with laughter. By his extraordinary velocity in running upstairs and his virtuoso performance in sliding down the banisters, Manley was able to answer the summons by bell or shout messages to people on the various floors of our house at almost the same moment.

From these early séances I learnt, in a somewhat dramatic manner, to use my powers of improvisation; these have since stood me in good stead. Often, in recent years, I have arrived at a studio sitting to find there are no backgrounds or properties with which to inspire me or my subject. On such occasions I employ the same technique as when I first took photographs in my home and used anything that came to hand, even if it were intended for some other purpose.

When I first started to take pictures, two towel racks balanced on chairs served as a support for half a dozen billiard cues from which fronds of gypsophilia or branches of Michaelmas daisies were hung on cotton thread. Beneath this precarious structure my sister sat on an upturned wastepaper basket in a grotto of American cloth. "You can't come in" was an anguished cry often heard when I was photographing, for the most peculiar objects were invariably placed against a door to form the outer structure of the picture on which my camera was trained. I am sorry that, for the sake of evidence, I have no snapshot to show the fantastic framework on which my romantic settings were built.

The weeks went by quickly and uneventfully while I continued living with my family on the north side of the park. Each month I had less and less idea what my ultimate profession was to be. I had accumulated some technical experience of photography, and when one or two acquaintances asked me to take their pictures I felt justified in claiming professional status. But the cash I received was forthwith spent in supplying myself with more photographic materials, and I made no profit. I was indeed fortunate not only to be living in comfort in my father's house but to have a small allowance.

Although my days were free from responsibility and should have been full of interest and excitement, they were also days of frustration. Stagnant and uninspired, I seemed helplessly incapable of solving my own problems. During my meanderings through London I had seen a house in St. James's

Tallulah Bankhead against a background of American cloth. My mother's drawing room is reflected in the ball. 1929.

Anna Mae Wong in a grotto of gypsophila and cellophane suspended from billiard cues

Square on one floor of which I imagined I would live while on another I would take photographs and on the top floor design for the theatre. But when I told my father of this ambition he did not encourage so grandiose a project. He was somewhat disappointed at the idea of my becoming a photographer. Had he given me this excellent education so that I should become a little man who climbed under a black velvet cloth and asked you to look at the dickey-bird? Yet after his first shock he agreed that if I were determined to take photographs he would allow me to begin in a "small way"; but nothing was decided, so I continued to take pictures at home, and Manley continued to carry the silver screen in and out of the conservatory.

Whereas I had imbibed my earliest interest in photography from the entirely commercial exponents in the field, I had since acquired higher ambitions. In imitation of some of the pictures in the London Salon of Photography, I photographed our aged Spanish cook, Isabel Villiegas, to look like a Rembrandt portrait; and, though the photography of landscape had little interest for me, I had taken my sisters as mere specks under some silver birches, as Corot might have painted them. But now I was in contact with new influences which showed themselves in my work. Diaghilev was giving a season of Russian ballet at His Majesty's Theatre. Marie Laurencin was exhibiting her pink-and-grey canvases at the Leicester Galleries. Next door was Boulestin's Restaurant, where I began to meet all sorts of people who encouraged my photography.

Curtis Moffat, whose abstract photographs and huge marbleised heads were extremely fashionable at this time, was friendly and encouraging, and I was extremely impressed by the flat lighting, or lack of lighting, and the compositions, or lack of composition, which he employed. In imitation of his work I hurried home to strip my sisters bare to the shoulders and bring my camera in so close to their faces as almost to touch their noses. I, too, bought a great variety of different-textured cardboards and coloured fancy papers on which to mount my Herculean enlargements; but my imitations never possessed the inimitable Curtis Moffat touch.

Another photographer whose work influenced me a great deal at this period was Francis Bruguière. His photography was entirely a question between himself and his camera. He did not photograph people, or everyday objects, caught at some dramatic moment or unusual angle. By using lights on strips of metal and paper, he created an abstract world which had, for me, a similarity with designs of the Russian ballet. Bruguière was not interested in imitating painting; he did not make imitation Corots of silver birches or rich Rembrandt portraits. He worked in a darkened room, cutting paper or metal sheets which he proceeded to paint with lights of varying intensity.

The results were a marriage of the camera and the essence of light. Although nothing dates more than a photograph (perhaps much of its charm lies in this fact), even today most of Bruguière's work remains remarkably dramatic in effect and timeless in quality.

Later I came under the influence of the work of Hoyingen-Huene, *Vogue's* star photographer in Paris. Huene, in his turn, had been under the spell of the great Steichen, but he brought more elaboration and extravagance to his photographs than the American master. Whereas Steichen seldom approached his subjects with humour, there was something almost frivolous in the way Huene brought a whole new collection of properties to his studios. Rich and illustrious women would play a losing game as they tried to keep their dignity against huge Corinthian columns, plaster casts of Hellenic horses' heads, heads of Greek gods, or plumes of pampas grass.

Huene was the first who used with taste the photographic enlargements of other photographs for his background, so that his models seemed to be disporting themselves among giant porcelain vases filled with gargantuan orchids. I think he was the first to photograph models lying on the floor below him, thus giving the effect of flying figures in a Greek frieze. Huene's violent activities in the pages of *Vogue* gave me my greatest incentive to rival his eccentricities. But, apart from climbing up ladders to photograph my sitters lying on the floor beneath, and turning the house upside down, I was not fully occupied.

After I had been living six months at home and doing very little apart from smoking Pera cigarettes and taking long hot baths, my father naturally became impatient. It was all very well for me to continue indulging my photographic whims upon my long-suffering family and a few friends, but he felt that by this time I should be supporting myself and earning my own living. It was true. I had by now come of age and had continued long enough idling on the allowance my father generously gave. My father's business as a timber merchant had never recovered from the aftereffects of the 1914–18 war, and I was living at a rate that he could ill afford. He was exasperated by my lack of plans and finally delivered an ultimatum that, unless I had found some means of support within the next six weeks, I must take up a position as clerk in his office in the City.

With such a possibility looming in the distance, I tried desperately to get a job doing some sort of decorative work. Charles B. Cochran was putting on a new revue, and when I took a portfolio of stage designs to him he gave me encouragement and asked me to submit ideas for two or three numbers he planned. I did my best. It was not very good, but I sent him the designs. Then I heard no more. Nor did I receive any other offers, except that Robert Her-

Lillian Gish

ring, a Cambridge friend, gave me the job of designing the jacket for his travel book on Andorra called *The President's Hat*. I painted a picture of a black felt hat under a Victorian glass dome and earned the sum of three guineas. Zero hour arrived, and early one Monday morning I went off to the City with my father.

The weeks that followed were almost the most baffling and depressing I have ever experienced. Lost in this cold, strange maze of the City, I had absolutely no idea what form of business was being transacted in the various ugly rooms that made up my father's office. Never having been any good at mathematics, I now faced enormous ledgers filled with figures demanding immediate attention. To add up five-figure columns would have taken me a month, and even if I had made a second attempt I should never have obtained the same result. I was panic-stricken; but a rather elderly clerk, like a character in a Thackeray novel, showed pity on me and tried to explain how I might employ his own patent adding process. With a gnarled finger he ran down the pages of figures like a human calculating machine and quaveringly recorded the total in a beautiful copperplate hand. I was filled with admiration. I, on the other hand, could not even write distinctly, for since my earliest schooldays I had imitated the handwriting of Lily Elsie or Gladys Cooper. So everything went wrong for me. I floundered and blotted the books with inkstains, and when this was discovered I was soon relieved of the ledgers. I was now put to some other task, but it involved typewriting, and I could not typewrite.

I was altogether incompetent—a complete fiasco. At luncheon in a sandwich bar I was equally out of my depth and had no idea what all these practical, average men in their black coats and pin-stripe trousers were talking about. I was, in short, a disastrous failure and I felt bitterly ashamed of myself.

My father quickly became aware that it was hopeless to keep me on in his office; I was merely an embarrassment to his clerks. So he arranged for me to go to the office of a Swedish friend, a Mr. Schmiegelow, who was to pay me one pound per week while I learned to use a typewriter and to send out invoices for sacks of cement. In this office I was shown much consideration and kindness, and I managed to spend many of my office hours learning to type, while writing letters to various publishers asking if I could call on them at some luncheon time in order to do book jackets for them, and enquiring incidentally whether they were interested in publishing fairy stories with photographic illustrations.

I collected some of my imitation Bruguière abstract photographs and the pseudo-Curtis Moffat heads, some stage designs, and put them in a portfolio. Sometimes the publishers summoned me to their offices, but these visits were depressing; the chance of work was small; when anything "turned up" they said they would inform me. I was treated with politeness, but my work, if of any value—which I was beginning to doubt—was not at all suitable for the average commercial publisher.

I spent many lugubrious months in Mr. Schmiegelow's office in Holborn, but I only really lived at the week end, or between or after office hours. In the midday interval, whenever I was not touting my portfolio around to publishers, I would forgo my lunch to eat a bar of chocolate in the reading room of the British Museum, intending to read ancient plays or look up books on costume. But I generally found that it took so long to get out the volumes that, before I had started to peruse them, it was time for me to return to my office desk and the cement sacks.

On Saturday afternoons I would give vent to my repressed enthusiasms by indulging in an orgy of photography. All the pictures I had stored in my mind during the week now tumbled into reality. The drawing room was again turned upside down, and the library and my bedroom as well. My sisters were disguised in Burnet materials as Duchesses of Malfi, Botticelli angels, or medieval nuns. At the end of the lengthy proceedings the floor was littered with bits of crumpled tinsel, battered lilies, torn silver paper, spools of film, and trodden make-up. Not only my sisters posed; by now a number of friends asked me to take their pictures professionally. One wanted a photograph for the frontispiece of his *Book of Poems,* and I would be given a fiver for it. Another was translating Pierre Louÿs, and would I care to do photographic illustrations? The publishers were an unknown firm and could not afford to pay much. But what about twenty-five pounds for six? I became very busy on Saturdays and Sundays.

By the end of one summer I had become so deflated by office life that I felt I could not continue. I was making no progress among the cement sacks, and time was racing on. I must succeed somewhere. I would speak to my father in the terms he understood.

"I'm being paid one pound a week at Mr. Schmiegelow's office," I said. "How can you ask me to remain there when I can make as much as that, or more, on a Saturday afternoon? If I stay at home and work I can certainly earn ten pounds a week." But my father said this was by no means certain.

In desperation I borrowed some money from a friend, went to Venice for a holiday, and wrote to my father saying that when I returned I would never enter the world of business again. Even if I were a failure I would devote myself to the arts. My father agreed sadly that I was of no use to anyone in any office in the City. I later discovered that he was giving Mr. Schmiegelow the one pound a week he was paying me to keep me in his employ.

Chapter 3 *FIRST SUCCESS*

I CAME back from my first visit to Italy in a somewhat more cheerful frame of mind. I had seen for the first time the silver beauty of Venice and had delighted in this world of opalescent marble, shining floors, and high Tiepolo ceilings. Perhaps the greatest excitement, however, had been my meeting with Diaghilev. At Florian's in the Piazza San Marco one evening I had showed the great man my stage designs. He had been quite polite. But now I was back in London, and the possibility of being asked to make theatrical designs seemed as remote as ever. I still had no plans. I had wasted six precious months in the City and I would not return there. I understood how unsuited I was to almost every ordinary job, and this gave me a feeling of inferiority and self-distrust which showed itself in many different ways. I became shy and inhibited, and if I had continued for long in this vein I should no doubt have become extremely embittered.

I was now twenty-two years old, and as each week passed I became more panic-stricken lest I should fail completely in adult life. Then one day a delightful and wise young friend said to me, "Don't worry so much about becoming anything very definite. Take it easy for a bit more and become a friend of the Sitwells." And, strangely enough, within a few weeks this was just what happened. Osbert Sitwell was amused by me, appreciative of my photographic efforts, considered my designs promising, and became a kind and helpful patron. He invited me to design the scenery for a play he and his brother had written, and encouraged his sister Edith, whom I now considered the most remarkable and beautiful-looking human object I had ever seen, to pose for me. With her etiolated Gothic bones, her hands of ivory, the pointed, delicate nose, the amused, deep-set eyes, and silken wisps of hair, I considered she must be more remarkable than any model that I would ever have the fortune to find.

Edith became a most willing subject for my camera. She posed wearing a flowered gown like Botticelli's Primavera; she sat on a sofa wearing a Longhi tricorne and looking like a Modigliani painting; she lay on the floor on a square of checkered linoleum disguised as a figure from a medieval tomb while I snapped her from the top of a pair of rickety house steps. At Renishaw Hall, the Sitwell house in Derbyshire, the ivy-coloured ruins, stone terraces ornamented with large Italian statues, and the tapestried rooms made wonderful backgrounds for pictures of her. Here was the apotheosis of all I loved. With an enthusiasm that I felt I could never surpass I photographed Edith playing ring-around-a-rosy with her brothers, plucking the strings of a harp, and wearing an eighteenth-century turban and looking like a Zoffany, as in a huge four-poster bed she accepted her morning coffee from a coloured attendant.

Suddenly I found myself busy taking all sorts of exciting photographs. All at once my life seemed fulfilled. New and wonderful friends seemed to appear from nowhere. Each week was full of opportunity. At last I was enjoying myself again. Although I had no money in the bank, I look back at this period, when luxury was comparatively cheap, as one of affluence. I was living comfortably at home, and the money that I happened to pick up for my photography, though not considerable, was spent in a very agreeable manner. By degrees I had begun to receive quite a number of cheques for the pictures that appeared in the magazines, and I was now able to indulge more riotously my fancies. Running amok among the theatrical fabrics at Burnet's store, I discovered materials for photographic backgrounds which created an extraordinary atmospheric effect of shimmer, like sunlight on water. I brought home yards of cotton fabric originally intended perhaps for circus performers, stamped with stars, polka dots, or stripes, and I bought tinsel of all textures. The backgrounds of my photographs at this period were often more important to me than the sitter, and I often painted special backgrounds of feathery trees, leaping fawns, or exotic flowers, so that my photographs looked as much like my designs as the camera would permit.

One day I decided I would like to have an exhibition of my photographs and, with complete faith in its ultimate success, I set about making a collection for a show. The Cooling Galleries in Bond Street were warmly hospitable. In one room there would be stage designs; in the other the enlargements of my snapshots, immaculately mounted, with my signature scrawled in red on the right-hand bottom corner of the mount.

My enthusiasm was now unquenchable and spread throughout my home. As more people arrived to be photographed for the exhibition, Manley, the butler, already overworked looking after our large family, was called in almost

Edith Sitwell photographed against a tapestry at Renishaw

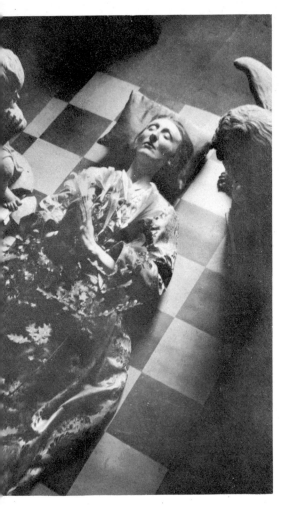

Edith Sitwell on a small strip of linoleum, photographed from a ladder by daylight. This was my first real success.

Edith Sitwell at Renishaw

Tilly Losch

every day to hold a heavy light over my sitter's head, so that I do not know when he found time to clean the silver. The front-door bell would ring—in fact, all the household bells rang—so frequently that Manley rushed up and down stairs with the pertinacity of a mechanical toy. Once his enthusiasm must have got the better of his judgment, for when Sacheverell Sitwell came to pay me a visit at teatime, the front door was opened and abruptly slammed in his face, while Manley panted out, "Down the back stairs, Sonny."

As the day of the exhibition approached, more and more distinguished people found time and the inclination to give me a last-minute sitting. The catalogue, for which Osbert Sitwell wrote a most delightful introduction, raced to and from the printer's with the latest additions and amendments.

In his flattering preface to the catalogue Osbert wrote, "Just as one other noted explorer, dropping all the paraphernalia of equatorial suits and sun hats, marched through the Central Forest of Brazil with bowler, umbrella, and blue serge suit, so, in his perilous voyage towards his discoveries, Mr. Cecil Beaton is armed with naught save a ladder, a tripod, and a Kodak." He described how, on the summit of the rickety ladder, I executed poses "worthy of a Blondin or of a Ducalion."

Ninnie, although now entirely superseded as family photographer, with great grace would stand by at sittings to shield a light or prop up a screen. She helped me to press the mounted photographs for the exhibition, championed me in the darkroom—now moved to the cellar—and even wrote out the envelopes for the invitations to the private view. But I rewarded her poorly. I became so overwrought and highly strung with staying up working day and night for a week on end that a member of the Sitwell family still talks with awe of my uncontrollable rage when Ninnie, on her way to the post office, stumbled and dropped the box containing the entire mountain of invitations into the gutter on a rainy London day.

The exhibition opened in a thick London fog. Yet somehow a surprisingly large number of people found their way to the Bond Street galleries. When Lady Colefax came in to see the show both in the morning and afternoon, I knew that everything was going well. I was the first photographer whose work caught the imagination of the general public. My unconventional pictures of celebrities—Tallulah Bankhead with a background of balloons, Tilly Losch in a tree trunk, Lady Milbanke under a glass bell—brought as much notoriety to me as to my sitters. Music-hall jokes were made about tramps going off to be photographed by Cecil Beaton; burlesques of my pictures appeared in the daily newspapers, and the weekly magazines competed with one another for my work. Mr. Hay Wrightson, a court photographer of considerable eminence in Bond Street, wrote an exceedingly gracious letter to congratulate me on the "artistry and originality" of my ideas, and to exclaim, "What a privilege to have not only a marvellous circle of friends, but courage to portray them in this bold and bizarre manner photographically."

On one of her yearly visits to England in search of talent Mrs. Chase, the American editor in chief of *Vogue* magazine, had seen some of my drawings. Mrs. Chase thinks she showed considerable perception in feeling that they showed promise and that they would one day be useful to her magazine. When she was told that I also took photographs I was summoned to her office to submit my work. Some of the pictures I showed her were stained, out of focus, or with heavy retouching discernible on the surface of the prints. They were obviously amateur work, but she said they were extremely personal and interesting. She would like me to take some pictures especially for her. "But," she asked, "have you a studio? Where is the developing done, and who does it for you?" She was amazed to hear a possible prospective staff photographer reply, "Oh, Ninnie does it in the bathroom." But Mrs. Chase was not entirely put off. "If you come to New York you must do some things for us."

The amateurishness of my methods continued to amuse her. The flimsy tripod I employed was always slithering on parquet floors. Not only was I obliged to make my sitters keep still a very long while, but I found it almost more difficult to prevent my camera from moving during the time exposures. One spidery leg of the tripod was weak and would frequently collapse; the camera would crash to the ground; the bellows would get bent out of line or the back case become jarred so that light leaked in. But I was undeterred by the existence of these self-imposed obstacles. To prevent the negatives from appearing mottled as if with clouds of cotton wool where the light had leaked through—knowing vaguely that red was the best color protection against daylight—I wrapped the camera in any red material that was at hand; the same red shirt that had become singed over the electric bulb when enlarging did double duty and now appeared as camera shroud. But it was so badly burnt that soon it fell to shreds and was succeeded by yards of peppermint-pink tarlatan (a discarded background) which now made a cocoon for the camera. The surprise with which my distinguished sitters met this strange-looking object cannot be exaggerated. Yet the proceedings never struck me as at all comic. With great intensity I would hold my breath during the long time exposures, praying that the pink cocoon would not tremble on the tripod, and, by prayer and determination, I triumphed over these very lively inanimate objects and got the results I wanted.

Paul Tanqueray was the only professional photographer I knew at this time. He was always generous in his encouragement of my work, and I shall never cease to be grateful to him for introducing me to a firm of technical experts who could bring the best out of my erratically exposed plates. Ever since my first delight and surprise at seeing such wonderful results from my negatives, my own enlarger became derelict, the gutta-percha baths and the packets of acids were thrown away, and my life became infinitely simplified, for Messrs. Jeffery & Boarder have continued to give me the greatest satisfaction ever since.

Chapter 4 A NEW WORLD

I N o w became ambitious to conquer new fields by going to America. I had only the vaguest indication of what life would be like in that world, but Beverley Nichols, who had enjoyed great success with his autobiography written at the age of twenty-five, described the enthusiastic welcome he had received in New York. So rosy was the picture he painted that I felt that I, too, must sample the delights of that glittering city.

"*Everyone* is so hospitable. *Everyone* asks you to stay. *Everyone* sends presents all the time. You come back to your rooms and find them *filled* with cardboard boxes of flowers," he said.

I did not realise that, since Beverley Nichols was a much-sought-after celebrity and I was an extremely shy and unknown young man who had only a handful of American acquaintances, my reception might not be comparable to his. However, armed with a pile of letters of introduction from Lady Cunard, and with a few hundred dollars in my pocketbook, I arrived at the Ambassador Hotel in New York in the middle of the winter season of 1928, when the boom was at its height and most people were so busy making money that they had little time for anything else. My cosmopolitan friend, Dr. Kommer, who hailed originally from Czernowitz and who spent his winters in New York, had advised me during his summer spent in London that, since rich Americans were often snobbish, I must stay in the best hotel; also that I must charge enormously high prices for my work.

I arrived terrified on the dock at New York, and the customs official asked if I had anything to declare. He looked extremely surprised when I showed him the contents of my trunks. I produced—still wrapped in its cocoon of pink veiling—the Kodak camera, the spidery tripod, the rather tarnished tinsel nets and silver tissues, the crumpled lengths of Burnet cottons, and the badly cracked American cloth which formed my backgrounds. Upon these things the success or failure of my career must rest. I had had, thus far, complete confidence that no one had ever seen anything like my glorious properties before and that they would bring me fame and fortune, but now suddenly they looked, even to me—proud of them as I was—shabby and forlorn. The customs official bid me go my way with an expression of contemptuous sympathy.

I arrived at the Ambassador Hotel, unpacked my properties, and sat down and awaited the ring of the telephone bell. Exactly who would telephone I did not know, but I felt "the Americans" must, by now, have somehow learned of my arrival. And surely they would start bombarding me with invitations. At any moment now the cardboard boxes of flowers must arrive. But nothing happened. For want of anything better to do, I took a bath. All the while I was lying in it my ear was cocked for the telephone bell. But it did not ring. I was too unadventurous to go forth from my room and explore the unknown twenty-eight floors below. It was dinnertime. With an effort I went downstairs to the hotel restaurant at an hour which was either late or early, for, apart from me, the place was empty, and, unable to withstand the stares of the waiters any longer, I went back to my room. Still no telephone calls. By degrees I grew sufficiently tired to fall asleep.

My New York existence started slowly, and the next few days provided a series of shocks and surprises not altogether pleasant. In reply to the letters of introduction I had delivered I was invited out to one or two meals; but at this time even the women were so busy playing the stock market that at luncheon time they were in such a hurry to make more money that they started to pull on their gloves as soon as coffee was ordered. I was much too shy and lacking in self-assurance to make any impression on people who, though quite willing to be kind, had very little time to waste.

For some weeks I was unable to get in a word edgeways; my timing was wrong and I found no opportunity to break into a conversation, for, even if the raconteur was eating, he would say, "Moreover," or "Whereupon," or "Now listen to this," before putting a piece of food into his mouth. I had much time on my hands and no spirit of adventure to help me overcome my timidity; in fact, it took me several days to summon up enough courage to go into a shop and buy a clothesbrush. However, one week after my arrival I returned from a museum to my hotel room to find a single large cardboard box on my bed.

"It's started!" I said to myself. "Success will be mine any moment now! At last the flowers I've heard so much about!"

But I opened the box to find it contained my laundry.

By slow degrees I began taking photographs in the sitting room adjoining

Mary Taylor in a fashion photograph

Princess Natalie Paley

my hotel bedroom which I had obtained especially for the purpose. New York prices at this time were at such a height that I could not afford to keep an extra room permanently; only when a sitting had been arranged was the communicating door unlocked for a charge of eighteen dollars. My photographic paraphernalia was constantly being moved back and forth.

I was thrilled by the beauty and elegance of many of my sitters; but my enthusiasm was somewhat dimmed by the fact that here in New York I knew of no firm of Jeffery & Boarder, and the technical side of my work caused me a great deal of anxiety. I could find no one to give personal attention to the developing of my films and the enlarging of my best negatives. Many an excellent picture was ruined by the crude mass-processing at the various photographic stores I frequented; the enlargements were coarse, mottled, with too much contrast, and totally unrecognisable as my work.

Just when I was beginning to despair I discovered an old man, who looked like a fur trapper, who spent his evenings making photographic enlargements of fine quality. When his cronelike wife, in an almost hairless fur coat exuding a strong ferrety odour, came to my hotel with a trial batch of her husband's Rembrandtesque versions of my negatives, my heart jumped with gratitude. Although the effects were not light and silvery as I had wished, at any rate they were prints of which I need not be ashamed. I gave the old man a large batch of negatives, and after a week he himself came to explain his difficulties. He could only undertake a limited amount of work, as he was slow to get good results and had to work late into the night. His wife always wanted him to work harder, but the pain in his back was becoming unbearable. I felt extremely sorry for him, driven on to further efforts by his domineering wife, having to stay up long after the world had gone to bed, and I knew only too well the pain in the back as one bends almost double over the various trays and basins. However, I had a duty to myself; the old man must provide me with good enlargements of my pictures of Mrs. Dodge-Sloane, Mrs. Walter Rosen, Mrs. Harrison Williams, Mrs. Morton Schwartz, Mrs. Lorraine McAdoo, Rosamond Pinchot, Carl Van Vechten, and other of my earliest New York sitters.

This strange old couple were very unreliable, and although they would promise pictures by a certain date, often it was impossible to track down either of them for many days at a time. Sometimes when I telephoned in anguish to know why the pictures had not arrived as promised I heard an incomprehensible shriek from the old woman, followed by the sound of the receiver slammed down. And then, special as these prints were, very special were the prices asked. I had by now spent all the dollars I had brought to the country and relied on any cheques coming in to pay the bills; but the fur

Fashion photograph

trapper's wife always insisted on being paid in cash on delivery, and sometimes this was difficult. At noon one day the husband arrived with a wonderful batch of long-awaited prints. The bill was excessively big, but by digging deep into my pockets I was able to pay. Two days later the wife arrived, screaming abuse and threatening me with her gnarled fist.

"You're crazy to pay that bit of old white trash for his woirk! I'm the one that takes the dough, or he goes off, gets drunk, and you get no more woirk!"

I soon learned that Dr. Kommer's advice had been sound and that it was never a wise thing in New York to sell one's work cheaply. By gulping hard and steeling my determination I decided to charge three hundred dollars for twelve of my photographs. When translated into English money this seemed a mighty sum, but at the end of each week it was very much "touch and go" whether I had been able to save much cash after the expenses of the processing of my pictures and the Ambassador Hotel bill had been paid. The noise—a swishing sound that I shall never forget—of the envelope containing the weekly bill being thrust under my door each Friday was a sound that struck terror into my heart.

Although I was starting to do some work for various monthly magazines, the contributors were paid for their work at the time of its publication, and at least six weeks elapsed before its going to press and its appearance on the newsstand. I felt it would be too humiliating to ask to be paid in advance. For several weeks my finances were at a very low ebb, and it was before the tide showed any signs of turning in my favour that I photographed the "great businesswoman."

"She is very rich," said a mutual friend who had arranged the sitting, but added, "She is also very difficult."

The businesswoman, a gigantic Juno—quite six feet tall—came to my hotel room with as much luggage as if she intended to stay for a week. Out of a gargantuan wardrobe trunk her maid proceeded to produce about a dozen evening dresses, and out of an even larger cabin trunk she unpacked a number of fur coats. After an hour and a half spent clicking the lens at my subject wearing a variety of dresses, I felt an interval of a few minutes for relaxation was necessary and I lit a cigarette.

"We mustn't delay!" I was told. "There are still a couple more evening dresses to do, and we haven't yet started on the furs!"

I took a number of pictures of my tormentor wrapped in an ermine coat; a great number more in a chinchilla coat. The sky outside my room had become dark. Most offices had closed for the day, but I must continue to work. I was by now somewhat exhausted, but still my Juno smiled at the camera with unflagging freshness. At last I admitted defeat.

"I am too tired to continue."

"Oh, but what about my sables!"

A few days later the negatives came back from the developer. I stayed up late nights retouching the pictures so that the tycoon looked like some little Kewpie doll. The pictures, when enlarged, were so basely flattering that I was almost ashamed to show them to the original, for surely self-deception could not go thus far! But the career woman was delighted. She smiled to let me see her dimples, and put her head to one side to show how closely she resembled the little coquette in my pictures. Then with businesslike precision she set about ordering the pictures in their dozens.

That evening I hardly dared tell the fur trapper the number of pictures I wanted him to enlarge for me. He would have to remain up at work throughout the nights for weeks upon end, and he was not interested in making large quantities of any one picture; he was an artist and wished to create only one or two exhibition prints; nor was he particularly interested in the money. I reckoned that, if he wished, on the proceeds he could escape from his wife and get drunk for weeks.

One morning the fur trapper's wife duly arrived with a mountainous wad of her husband's masterly enlargements of the businesswoman. I took a quick look at them.

"Yes! They are superb prints!"

The fur trapper was a genius. The business executive would be thrilled to see herself in all her glory.

"But couldn't the entire lot be a bit cheaper? There are so many of them."

"No."

"Well, I *do* see they are wonderful prints, but you know it's rather difficult for me to pay all this out at once."

She retreated towards the door with the prints under her arm.

"Why didn't you say so before? When you raise the dough, I'll leave the pictures—not before."

Eventually the prints were in my possession. I pasted the backs of the prints, placed them on cardboard, and flattened them under books on which I placed the legs of chairs in my hotel bedroom. Finally, with my proud signature scrawled in red paint, the mounted pictures were sent off.

Ten days later I was summoned to the businesswoman's headquarters. As I went through the labyrinth of corridors I felt a little more nervous than usual. Finally I reached a circular room decorated in becoming shades of grey, and in the centre of it stood the six-footer. I could soon tell that the atmosphere was tense. Her employees stood around as if completely numbed. Madame obviously had been giving them hell, and they knew there was possibly more to come. At Madame's side was the familiar mountain of my hand-mounted trapper's prints. Madame took the top picture off the pile and held it towards me.

"What is this, Mr. Beaton?" she roared.

"How do you mean? It's one of your photographs."

"Do you think I look like that?" The face, so contorted with rage, in no way resembled the lady in my pictures.

"Well—er—yes—er—no—well . . . You said they were very good."

"Well, I just don't look anything like that. It's an insult! Look at me there. It's disgraceful to make me look old and ugly."

"Oh no! Not old and ugly! So young!"

"I don't like them at all!"

"But you liked them so much——"

"Yes, I did, but the proofs were quite different."

"They're exactly the same. You can compare them——"

"They're not the same! And I'm not going to have them. You can take the lot back."

She then started to bellow and stamp and tear up some of the pictures, while many of the others went hurtling through the air like quoits. The bystanders stood transfixed. I was unable to utter a word before leaving.

This was the one occasion during my first visit to America when a sitter was not enthusiastic about the results of my work. In later years I met this same businesswoman at a cocktail party. She was a little drunk and bore down upon me with her face somewhat flushed.

"Oh, Mr. Beaton, have you forgiven me? We all make mistakes—and I admit I made a mistake. But I wish you'd do some work for me. You give all the women such a lovely ethereal look—so petite. It's just what I need for myself." I agreed it was.

Meanwhile, the sitting-room door adjoining my room at the Ambassador became unlocked more and more often, until finally I had accumulated such a mass of photographs and paraphernalia that the room became permanently mine. My sitters were extremely helpful and kind, and my heart began to glow with appreciation of life in New York.

I showed my latest photographs to Mrs. Chase, who considered that, although they might be poor technically, they had the merit of being unlike the pictures of any other photographer. I was soon taken into the *Vogue* fold and commissioned to photograph beautiful women up at Condé Nast's fabulous apartment on Park Avenue. That I should receive payment for the opportunity to photograph in such settings, with the assistance of proper electrical equipment and electricians to tend the lights, was like being given a pass to photograph in the Elysian fields. And how beautiful these women were who came to be photographed, with their sleekly shingled hair, their huge solitaire diamond rings, choker pearl necklaces, in their knee-length dresses with waistline at the hip level, and possibly a felt cloche hat that snuffed out all the features of their faces except the large pouting mouth.

Edward Steichen was the Almighty Photographer at this time. His rich and meticulous studies, so full of character, so full of light and shade, were now covering the pages of *Vanity Fair* and *Vogue*. But, much as I admired Steichen's work—and I used to examine his prints with absorbed curiosity— I knew that it would be hopeless for me ever to try to work in his vein. My work was the opposite end of the photographic pole, and the success of my first published pictures was partly due to their divergence from the Steichen tradition. Whereas Steichen's pictures were taken with an uncompromising frankness of viewpoint, against a plain background, perhaps half black, half white, my sitters were more likely to be somewhat hazily discovered in a bower or grotto of silvery blossom or in some hades of polka dots.

Mrs. Carroll Carstairs, Janet Newbold, Ina Claire, Gertrude Lawrence, Beatrice Lillie, Fred and Adele Astaire, and others came to be photographed by me in Mr. Nast's drawing room with the Chinese paper which came from Haddon Hall, in his mirrored dressing rooms where I was always so impressed to see each day fresh bunches of lilies of the valley in the mirror vases, in his salon with the Coromandel screen, Savonnerie carpet, and French drawings, or in his English-walnut library.

Some of my sitters looked at my photographic equipment with a certain distrust, and certain magazine editors accompanying me to the photographic sessions confessed that it was sometimes hard to convince their fashionable sitters, accustomed to being taken by vast and wonderful technical equipment, that they were not being palmed off with a makeshift sitting. Carmel Snow, now editor of *Harper's Bazaar*, relates how she met with great difficulty in reassuring the sitters that they were not being made fools of by me, manipulating a "child's camera," and that the pictures would be "perfectly lovely." Nowadays no one is surprised to see small Leicas and Rolleiflex cameras produced for an important photographic occasion; Mrs. Snow considers this was the beginning of what she terms "the small-camera era."

Perhaps I still thought of photography in terms of the days when I was taking pictures in my own home; when in order to give in my picture an effect of luxury I would buy one single lily. But the extravagant cost of a fashion sitting, lightly borne by the magazine, never failed to delight me.

"You want some white flowers?" an editor would enquire.

"Of course—if we may . . ."

"We'll send down to the florist for them right away. Do you want more than a dozen bunches? You want some tapestry? Or a Louis XVI canapé?"

When Alfred Lunt and Lynn Fontanne first came to be photographed by me they seemed amazed to watch the battle which I waged before them with my ungainly tripod as it slipped on the marble floor. But in spite of all set-backs, I managed to take successful pictures of them sitting at the piano with their reflections in the polished lid, with their heads seen in seven or eight different poses on the same picture; and although I photographed Mr. and Mrs. Lunt on many happy occasions during the years to come, I feel that during that afternoon's work the results were better than at any other time. Quite recently the Lunts described to me this first afternoon session, which was to develop into a true and lasting friendship.

"We were so surprised," said Lynn, "to find this young man, whose work had met with such success in London, had so little confidence."

"You were almost trembling with shyness," added Alfred.

"We couldn't get fascinated by you," continued Lynn. "You were *much* too shy. We were also surprised that there was absolutely nothing professional about your equipment. In fact, after being photographed so often by Mr. Steichen, we were rather shocked! We expected from *Vogue* magazine the last word in art! But although your paraphernalia was so unprofessional, we thought the whole procedure peculiar and interesting, and the thing that interested us was that, in your own way, you were so efficient. You knew exactly what you wanted to photograph and set about it in a most direct and businesslike manner."

"And of course," said Alfred, his eyes wild with serious intensity, "it was the first time we had been photographed at such peculiar angles!" He grimaced. "Suddenly you climbed up a ladder with your camera and, holding your breath for a long exposure, photographed us from above, sitting at the piano and showing just the tops of our heads, and then you came down to earth again and shot at us from underneath the music rest of the piano, showing nothing but our chins!"

Lynn added, "And I remember a few winters later, when for the first time we saw your drawings, I said to you, 'How old are you?' 'Twenty-six,' you said, and I exhorted you to stop all this nonsense of photography right away and to stick to drawings, and you said, 'Oh, but I must continue with it just for the time being, but I promise you I'll not be taking photographs in five years!'"

At no stage of my photographic career could I ever have believed that photography could be my life's work. It was a fascinating hobby, made much more fascinating by the cheques I received for my efforts; but I felt I had be-

Gertrude Lawrence

Ina Claire. An attempt to use studio props to achieve a surrealist effect.

Alfred Lunt and Lynn Fontanne

Alfred Lunt and Lynn Fontanne

come a professional photographer quite by accident. As the years went by I was appalled to realise how large a proportion of my time photography had taken. But the new type of photographer had suddenly sprung into being and was much in demand. I could not resist offers when my work was done so spontaneously and needed no moments of quietness and meditation; the quick-fire results seemed suited to the restless life I began to lead in the world's great capitals.

My first photographic assignment on a New York stage was when photographing Ruth Gordon, who was appearing in an enchanting production of *Serena Blandish*. After the matinee I climbed onto the stage with my Kodak. Star, stage manager, publicity men, electricians, and stage crew looked on in amazement as I battled with the tripod, which on this particular occasion refused, more obstinately than ever, to hold itself aloft. Miss Gordon later told me that she considered herself the victim of a stage-struck youth who merely wished to have a glimpse behind the scenes. Never for one moment did she believe that my performance would bring forth any results, and she was dumfounded when six weeks later, in *Vanity Fair* and *Vogue*, she saw full-page photographs which, she said, not only showed herself to great advantage but also gave quite a good suggestion of the vast expanses of black-and-silver American-cloth curtains, the far-flung chandeliers, and the large bunches of lilies of Robert Edmond Jones's brilliantly imaginative stage settings.

Soon I had photographed a sufficient amount of New York celebrities to make an exhibition. Hoping to emulate the success of the London show, I looked around for possible galleries; but it was difficult to find one available at short notice. However, one Elsie de Wolfe—Lady Mendl—whom I had met through Elisabeth Marbury, generously offered me the use of her interior-decoration establishment on Fifty-seventh Street. If I would care to show my pictures among her pieces of decoration and furniture, she would give me her support.

This show did not cause as much of a stir as the one in London, but it helped to make my American reputation. From that time on all sorts of persons sat for me. By the end of my New York visit not only had I provided the fur trapper and his wife with enough money for them both to retire on, and incidentally lined my own pockets, but I brought home a contract with the Condé Nast Publications to take photographs exclusively for them for several thousand pounds a year for several years to come. When I told my Father this news, he looked puzzled and scratched the back of his head disbelievingly, murmuring, "It sounds all right, but is it?"

Chapter 5 *THE EARLY THIRTIES IN LONDON, CHICAGO, NEW YORK, AND HOLLYWOOD AND MORE TRAVEL ABROAD*

BACK in London I now had a notion to publish a modern *Book of Beauty*. It was to be in imitation of the Victorian albums in which lovely young ladies swooned over doves, read love letters, or admired trails of convolvulus while they faced a page of glowing descriptive text. This contemporary version was to be illustrated with my photographs and ornamented with purple prose written by myself. Today it is strange to think that any publisher should have been willing to undertake so expensive a volume and one so limited in popular appeal, but the enthusiasm of Thomas Balston of Messrs. Duckworth was well rewarded; the book proved to be a *"succès de scandale."*

Society ladies had not before been seen posing with their heads under a Victorian glass dome, peering through broken tinsel screens, or lying head to head on the floor. Although the subjects themselves were content to be presented in this manner, their rivals did not hesitate to voice their resentment. Some of the photographs were considered extremely undignified. An angry father wrote to me that the photograph of his daughter was "most unsuitable." Certain gentlemen in St. James's Street club windows waxed purple with rage at the manner in which I chose to describe their womenfolk; and, for some undiscoverable reason, although she had given me every help and encouragement with the book and was flattered that I should include her among my favourites, my friend Lady Cunard, in a fit of pique, burnt the book at a luncheon party, running it through with a red-hot poker and lamenting, "He's a low fellow, and it's a terrible book!" No doubt it was a terrible book, but I was thrilled to think I had produced it. When the reviews I had awaited during sleepless nights eventually appeared, they were provocative and violent.

Next winter, while staying in New York, I was summoned to Chicago, where one of the city's most active lights, Mrs. Howard Linn, had the idea of producing for a charity performance a series of *tableaux vivants* taken from my *Book of Beauty*. That anyone in Chicago should have heard of my book surprised me, for it was never published in the United States. I was met at the station early one morning by the leading personages in the entertainment and, without being given time to shave, was whisked to the theatre where my photographs were being brought to life. I have seldom been more amazed. Here, thousands of miles from my home, was a whole group of strangers dressed as my sisters or as my close friends.

"Forward, Miss Baba Beaton," somebody shouted, and there stepped forth a young lady, somewhat plumper than my sister, but wearing a replica of her dress of Burnet's silver tissue and pearls; in imitation of the lilies I had bought from the man with a basket at the corner of Grosvenor Square, she held a bunch of lilies faithfully copied by Chicago's Smidt's Costume shop.

"Forward, Lady Lavery." And in imitation of the four-headed exposures I had made of my beautiful sitter in London, four Chicago hostesses, their faces painted black and white, put their heads through four slits in a plush velvet cloth.

"Now then ,for Miss Edith Sitwell." I was amazed when a gaunt and obviously sporting young lady lay down on an exact copy of my homely strip of checked oilcloth and clasped her hands in a timeless sleep.

"Come on, Tallulah Bankhead!"

"Hi there, Marchesa Casati!"

"Now then, Lady Diana Cooper! Not so fast! Remember you're the Madonna!"

When Mrs. Linn started to recite through a megaphone the deathless prose I had concocted to accompany the photographs of my beauties, my embarrassment was acute.

I am bound to admit that the final performance was considered to be a failure, for the Chicago audience had no idea of what the entertainment was about. I myself felt that fame had at last come to me in a most unaccountable and disturbing way.

The number of people who wished to be photographed by me increased in avalanche fashion. In London I continued to take photographs in my mother's drawing room, where the difficulties never seemed to dampen my ardour, and my sitters would find themselves embowered in flowers, real and artificial mixed, in cellophane clouds, or in balloons. The atmosphere of the early Daly's Theatre musical comedies, with their artificial rambling roses, tree borders of laburnum, wisteria, and chestnut blossom, with the pastel "colour schemes by Comelli," the ladies in chiffon Empire gowns embroidered with opalescent sequins, still had an influence on my photographic taste,

Princess Kapurthala

and even to this day those first childhood visits to the theatre are repaying their dividends of nostalgic emotion.

It was a milestone in my career as a photographer when, one happy afternoon, Lily Elsie, the lady who had first inspired my interest in photographing beautiful women, was herself to come to sit for me.

I awaited with nervous anticipation the arrival of my leading lady, who, as all leading ladies should, arrived a few minutes late. When she appeared, standing hesitantly in a doorway, I stood electrified. Her "entrance" was quite magical. Lithe and spruce, she walked with a slightly coltish walk, and the features of that lovely face had triumphantly stood the test of time. "This is not the beauty that one sees in the greatest paintings," I later considered. "But Boucher, Greuze, and Burne-Jones would have essayed to portray the liquid melting eyes, the cherry quality of the lips, and the ivory volutes of the nostrils."

As I looked at the sweet expression that defied the slight coarseness of the features, I felt a strange thrill of familiarity. The eyes were like large pools reflecting the sad blue of twilit sky. How well I remembered all the various details of her rounded beauty; how little I had forgotten! How well I knew, from the early postcards, that little lump almost hidden in the crevice by the left nostril, and, accenting the rosebud effect, the small boss in the centre of the upper lip. Completely fascinated, I watched the astonishingly pretty effect of the way the mouth moves in speech; the lips, so smooth and shining, are thrust forward into a sort of open pout which reveals the slightly receding teeth; the nose is beautifully placed on the face, and the head proudly carried on the column-like neck. Years after I had first seen her picture postcard lying on the counterpane of my mother's bed, Miss Lily Elsie, long since retired from the stage, still possessed an extraordinary power of magnetism.

That afternoon I tried to capture the aura of romance and excitement in which my heroine had always appeared to me. I found that the artificial, rather hard electric lighting which it was my custom to use was less suited to registering these carefully modulated features than the soft lighting of Rita Martin's daylight studio. So after a while I started to take pictures of my sitter in the small conservatory at the back of the drawing room. I had discovered in the attic of a charming elderly milliner an original hat of the "Merry Widow" period. It was a huge affair of white muslin, with a large crown made entirely of muslin roses. I asked Miss Elsie if she would wear this for me. The hat was immediately sent for, and when Miss Elsie put it on it was as if time had stood still. Although since I had first admired her I had become acquainted with the paintings of Piero della Francesca,

Greco, Blake, had discovered the Russian ballet, and admired many strange and wonderful people, yet in spite of all I had seen in the intervening years, although her hair was threaded with white and was curled in the fashion of the moment, this phenomenon in front of my camera still managed to create the everlasting quality of youth and loveliness.

Each winter I returned to New York to take photographs with a passionate enthusiasm. I was utterly contented with my work, which I felt to be important and a contribution to the general scheme, and was happier than I had been at any other time of my life.

Condé Nast took an avuncular interest in me and my photography, and if he felt there were any special feminine *bonne bouches* for me to photograph he would send them along. Every now and then he would call me to his office to criticise a batch of my latest pictures. Some of my enlargements were mottled and grained, and these defects became exaggerated when reproduced in the magazines. As he fingered his way through the black-and-white prints he reaffirmed his oft-repeated opinion, "What we want is colour! Now this is so flat and grey. There's too little contrast and no definition." But on one particular morning he had further guidance for me. "It's all very well for you to take pictures with a snapshot camera, but you've got to grow up! Don't you realise you're giving yourself so much unnecessary trouble by not having good technical equipment? Now you've got to go off and buy yourself a big camera to take pictures on an eight-by-ten plate."

I was appalled; I argued; I put up every obstacle. "I won't be able to get the background as sharp as the subject's face—which is one of the reasons my pictures have such a pleasant texture; my work will look like a real cameraman's!"

But Mr. Nast stood firm.

I played my last card. "Why, with a great heavy cumbersome camera," I wailed, "I won't be able to climb up ladders!"

"At any rate," Mr. Nast replied, "the pictures you take on the ground will be better." And he tried to comfort me by explaining that, once I had become accustomed to using a professional photographic apparatus, I would be grateful to him for precipitating the change; I could get so many other effects with a better lens. "I am not going to give you the camera. You just go off on your own and buy one."

I did not quite know why he did not give me the camera, and I was more than ever disgruntled that I had to spend precious dollars from my savings. I bought, however, a huge camera fitted with the same lens, so I was told, that Mr. Steichen used, and next day I travelled to Hollywood.

Gary Cooper. An early Hollywood photograph, using studio background.

Johnny Weissmuller, taken in a Hollywood studio

Orson Welles

The editor of *Vanity Fair* had wired the publicity staffs of the leading motion-picture firms that I was to take pictures of their principal stars, and every possible aid was lavished on me. From the telephone came a stream of invitations to the various studios. Cars were put at my disposal for as long as I wanted them. I was given as many assistants as I needed, with a couple of "prop" men to carry my equipment around the lots.

Now, after twenty years' experience of finding to what lengths some people will go to try to induce me to take free publicity photographs, it may here strike the reader that I was perhaps a little naïf to be so flattered by the attentions of the various public-relations officers representing the many film companies. Today I would certainly find these onslaughts somewhat tiresome. But I was still comparatively new to the game; I had infinite enthusiasm and energy, and Hollywood possessed mystery for me. When first I arrived I was thrilled at the offers of cars, cafeteria lunches, et cetera.

My first impressions of a film studio were so strange and fantastic that I felt I could never drain their photographic possibilities. The vast sound stages, with the festoons of ropes, chains, and the haphazard impedimenta, were as lofty and awe-inspiring as cathedrals; the element of paradox and surprise was never-ending, and the juxtaposition of objects and people gave me my first glimpse of surrealism. I discovered that the dressing rooms of the stars were built with façades of various nationalities and styles, so that when necessary they could be used for background for films of England, Holland, Germany, and Russia. Many of the buildings on the film lot had no insides to them, and few were four-sided. Everywhere there was a most extraordinary mixed population of medieval beggars, executioners, Negroes in crinolines, and ladies in full evening dress of the 1914 period.

I could take my choice of sitters—Carole Lombard, Norma Shearer, Gary Cooper, Marion Davies, Joan Crawford—almost anyone I wished, with the exception of the Great Garbo, who, I was told, was on holiday in the mountains. This was a sad disappointment, as she, more than all the others, was the one I wished to meet. Another shade on my happiness was my brand-new camera. I hated the cumbersome thing; I felt rooted to the earth with it; I could not assert my domination over it; there were so many complicated stops to compete with, and I never knew just how the results would come out.

My first sitter happened to be Clive Brook. He was already made up and waiting for me when I arrived, late, with my heavy apparatus. Although I took a long while in preparing for the ordeal, he was quite patient with me. Nevertheless, he registered surprise when I pulled out one of the slides from the back of the camera and asked him if he knew how the damn thing worked. Guesswork was still my method. I had no meter to read for the correct exposure, and, considering how vague I was about the whole procedure, it is surprising that my new negatives came out as well as they did.

For the first few days in Hollywood I cursed Condé Nast under my breath each time I had to make an exposure with my beastly camera. To have to abandon my old snapshot camera and start with my new apparatus was like having to walk with a wooden leg after an amputation. For some time the results with the new lens were as prosaic and impersonal as I feared they might be. I was extremely depressed. But when at last I took a close-up of Janet Gaynor lying in a field of wild flowers and every detail of the smallest chickweed was seen with incredible clarity, I realised there were, after all, some advantages in working with this type of instrument. By degrees I became accustomed to the new working conditions, and my poor battered No. 3A Folding Pocket Kodak, wrapped in its red muslin, fell into disuse.

Hollywood architecture fascinated me, and I made a photographic record of the Hansel and Gretel Kindergarten School for girls and boys, the Dandy Eats Restaurant, and only the dim but hardly religious light prevented me from photographing Aimee Semple McPherson, the "Hot Gospeller," in her church with its bawdyhouse decorations, where the angels in the stained-glass windows looked like show girls.

It was on the Universal set that I had my first glimpse of war. *All Quiet on the Western Front* was being filmed. The California sun had not shone for several days; in fact, rain had fallen so heavily that mud and slush were ankle-deep. A wrecked French village, complete with church, looked so realistic that one could not believe one was in the midst of a papier-mâché make-believe. There were hundreds of unshaven soldiers sitting about, swearing and grumbling.

Soon after I arrived on the lot an assistant director, George Cukor, arranged that I should be taken up in a crane to view, from the skies, the scene that was about to be taken. A battalion of soldiers under fire ran through the mud, while explosions, raising fountains of earth, took place around them. At a given moment a cloud of flame flashed and, to the accompaniment of an ominous roar, a crash of splintering metal, and a tom-tom rattle of breaking trees, the church was blown into the air. The crane on which I was perched shook so violently that I was almost precipitated to the ground. Movie cameras were busily grinding away, the ambulance was in readiness, but the only casualty was the director, whose nose and eyes were cut by flying fragments.

When the "take" was over and I returned to ground level, blinding fierce lights were reset in the ruined village, and I photographed a nice and hitherto unknown young man named Lew Ayres, who was being given the opportunity of his life by playing the much-coveted leading role. Louis Wolheim, the character actor, a great big tough with a broken nose, shaven head, and unshaven jowl, was sitting on a half-destroyed well head, looking so alarmingly brutal that I quaked at the prospect of approaching him with the camera. But I was told Wolheim was a professor and the most learned, cultivated person in the film colony. I was therefore surprised to hear a stream of four-letter words pour from between his broken yellow teeth.

Each day brought more solicitations from the publicity staffs of the picture companies; and the only star who could not be corralled for me was Greta Garbo. Miss Garbo was, as half the world knows, averse to publicity and elusive as quicksilver. However, the Metro-Goldwyn-Mayer publicity department was enthusiastic about the pictures I had already taken of their other leading stars, and they tried their best to inveigle Miss Garbo to the studio on my behalf. For days I was kept on tenterhooks.

Herewith an extract from a diary:

It is really too awful that she is so evasive. I have pulled a hundred wires to try to see her, to photograph her, to draw her, but without success, and everywhere I go I hear of her beauty and intelligence. Today Mother Janis heaped on torments, one after another, about Garbo's movements being more beautiful than a panther's, her skin more ivory than ivory, teeth more pearly than pearls, and eyelashes which, when her eyes looked down, spread across her cheeks like a peacock's tail. She is the only star with glamour, and she is a hermit. They talked so much about her today that I became quite sick with unrest, so that Elsie, taking her courage in her hands, went out and very kindly telephoned, but she soon came back. "Mees Gareboh ees awaye fo week end."

At lunch today in the Metro-Goldwyn canteen, Howard Strickling of the publicity staff plied me with information about Garbo. He would do his best to see if anything could be done about my photographing her, but when she first came to Hollywood she was photographed for publicity with pigs and dogs and horses and dolls, and she hated it. She said that when she was a star she would not be photographed with pigs and horses and dogs and dolls, and now she is a star of the greatest magnitude. She is pleased and flattered that she is this amazing success, but she does not want to meet her fans. Women send orchids to her every day, men telephone on long-distance calls to try to hear her voice, but she does not give a damn and the fact that she doesn't give a damn and will not come out of her hiding only increases the frenzy.

My day was exciting, for news of the chances of my photographing her kept trickling through, and by midday I was jubilant, for instead of the chances being 1000 to 1 against, they were now 6 to 1. Strickling had spoken to Garbo on the telephone. She said she did not know about it. Oh well!

For days on end I was waiting expectantly for a summons. At last, the day before I was leaving, and with high hopes, I telephoned to Strickling for a final effort. "Not a chance! But we've lined up Shearer for you!"

As it happened, that night I had the delicious pleasure of meeting Greta Garbo for the first time. The circumstances in which we found ourselves were congenial, even romantic. We became friends, and I was quite enthralled by this legendary creature. I had never imagined such beauty was possible. All that I had heard of her from Mrs. Janis and others was nothing compared to this incredible-looking person with the pale Débureau face dressed in white sports clothes. I would cancel all my plans if she would permit me to stay and photograph her.

"No, no! Tomorrow I work," she said sadly.

The next morning I left Hollywood.

My Hollywood photographs were widely published and had a great influence in the film capital. Instead of photographing that small oasis of artificiality, the painted set in the centre of the studio—a set generally so ugly and bereft of life—for the first time someone had turned his camera on all the mechanics of the studio; the asbestos-lined doors, the scaffolding, the festoons of chains and electric wires, the back sides of the sets. For some time afterwards I was amused to see, in the fan magazines, pictures of stars resting against a carefully placed arc light, or idling by a mountain of tin film cans; and though I was flattered by these imitations, I was relieved that only superficially did they resemble my work.

Condé Nast's policy of publishing in his magazines photographs taken exclusively for him led inevitably to the establishment of a Condé Nast studio.

The first of these studios was organised in Paris. When I first went to Paris to take photographs in the Condé Nast studio I began to wonder if, after all, I had any claim to call myself a photographer; without my own properties, camera, and equipment, I felt entirely at a loss. As a result of my Harrow education I could speak only a few words of French, and on arrival at the studio I was nonplussed to see such a wonderfully equipped inferno of machinery with which to work. To give orders to my French assistants in front of my French sitters was acutely embarrassing.

My first subject, I was told, was to be a very interesting woman. Colette would be here at three o'clock this afternoon, but I had not yet read any of Colette's books. This strange being, looking like a marmoset, glanced at me ferociously. Her eyes darted around the place; she jabbered; she raised her shoulders at me, then in desperation raised the palms of her hands. I

A Tunisian

was baffled to know what to do with her. I did not then recognise her strange and very particular beauty, did not understand her personality, and she did not seem ready to help me in my predicament. I was inexperienced, and my artistry failed me. I tried to make her good-looking, to flatter her in the conventional way—a hopeless task. The pictures were very bad.

But gradually I became accustomed to working conditions in the French office, and soon Condé Nast studios were also opened in London and New York. Without assuming any of the responsibilities of running an expensive studio of my own I was now able to experiment under ideal technical conditions in the Nast laboratories at almost any season of the year.

At this time George Huene showed me some of his recent photographs taken in Tunisia.

"All these pictures were taken with a Rolleiflex camera," he said. "It's a most simple and useful little machine. The negative is just big enough to enlarge to almost any size. I'll get you one if you like."

I took George Huene's advice. With our Rolleiflexes we went off together on a photographic trip to North Africa, far into the desert. This was my first essay at taking travel pictures, and I have to thank Huene for having enlarged my photographic range. Although the results of my Tunisian trip were far less successful than Huene's, they encouraged me to continue; and I now consider my travel photographs an important and interesting part of my photographic output.

Ever since this trip I have used the Rolleiflex camera; it is an all-weather camera which can be employed on almost every occasion and is so simple to manipulate that the handling of it becomes automatic. It is a great advantage to be able to see the composition one is about to take in the ground glass; its sole disadvantage to me is that it has no adjustable back, so that if one tilts the camera up at high buildings there is considerable distortion, and the lines which should be horizontal converge as if in an earthquake.

By now my annual output of pictures was prodigious. My summer holidays were always taken abroad, and I reaped such a rich photographic harvest that I would come home with my suitcase bulging with packets of negatives all waiting to be made into glorious enlargements. I spent one halcyon holiday photographing in Provence, where the light, so soothing and lingering, seems more beautiful perhaps than anywhere else in the world. Aix was a particular enchantment with its dove-coloured buildings, its double arcades of lime trees, silvery stone statues, the scent of wood fires, acacia blossom, hay, herbs and manure, and, at night, the theatrical effect of the lights among the overhanging branches. The garden at Nîmes is one of the loveliest

A Moroccan street

Ouled-Naïls in a brothel in Fez

Corsican fishermen mending a net. The background is the wall of a house.

I have known, though its peaceful atmosphere has never been successfully captured by my camera.

The holiday snapshots might also include pictures of idyllic picnics on emerald-green grass slopes in Switzerland, of glimpses of Wagnerian mountain passes in Germany, or the lush pinewoods and musical-comedy-like Austrian villages with petunias billowing over window boxes or rickety staircases. Sight-seeing tours among the strange whimsies of the mad Ludwig of Bavaria influenced my work during the winter months.

My first arrival in Rome was perfectly staged, for it was twilight—the loveliest light of the day—and all the populace was gazing excitedly into the sky to see the planet Venus. Some *festa* was being celebrated, and horses and carts were decorated with bright colours and tinsel flowers; the black-garbed priests who hurried along were in contrast to the general atmosphere of gaiety and to the lightness of the scene. Under our windows children in blues, greens, pinks, and scarlet played mysterious games with green spear-leaved branches of bamboo, while nearby the fountains plashed refreshingly.

Almost every winter I would use Manhattan as a jumping-off place and would embark upon some sight-seeing, photograph-collecting tour—to the Bahamas, the West Indies, or to Mexico. The elaborate Churrigueresque architecture of Mexico with its worm-mold decorations, the brilliant gilded interiors of the churches with the dazzling patterned tilework, the mounds of fiesta masks, and the paper flowers in the villages were a source of constant satisfaction; and when spring came I would return to England with an enormous batch of pictures. There I photographed with renewed enthusiasm until the month of August, when once more I would be off on my travels photographing the marshmallow beauty of the Arab quarter in Morocco or the blue mosques in Turkey. During a cruise to Athens and the Greek islands I reaped a rewarding photographic harvest.

Here is an extract from my diary written in the late thirties marked "End of April":

After many last-minute postponements I have at last sailed from Manhattan en route for home. Each time I have planned to leave New York I have realised I couldn't possibly get through all the photographs I had contracted to take, and so another postponement was made which, in its turn, brought further commitments. Although generally I must have ten hours sleep per night in order to keep going, I have lately managed to feel extremely well with five, though, when anything goes wrong, I am likely to become somewhat hysterical. But it has been the most enjoyable winter; I can never think of when I was consistently happier, or at least when I had less unhappiness. Now I feel con-

Magnolias

Lilacs at Ashcombe

fident, at last, that I can ward off that which I dreaded most in New York—loneliness. Now if there is an empty evening it is with relief that I remain busy in my room attending to a thousand things that should have been done, or else simply getting back strength by sleep.

At this time I rented on a long lease Ashcombe, a very remote and romantic house situated among the most beautiful woods in the Wiltshire Downs. Having spent much love and energy and all my money on its decoration, I felt I had transformed it into the ultimate of beauty. With its pale light colours and silver ornamentation indoors and its ilex trees, stone garden ornaments, and high surrounding line of downs, it was an ideal setting for photography. As the year progressed I photographed the May trees in blossom, the old lilac sprawling over the kitchen-garden wall, the Caroline Testout roses, the statues decorated with garlands of flowers and more bucolic scenes, the new chicks seen between the spokes of the farm cart wheel, the evening's count of eggs placed on an old tree stump.

My guests were often chosen for a week-end visit for their photogenic qualities. Tilly Losch would arrive bringing with her the costume of a Meissen shepherdess, to be photographed in our valley amidst a herd of terrified sheep; Princess Paley brought some beautiful black costumes which Oliver Messel had designed for her to wear in the film *Don Juan;* Ruth Gordon produced her wardrobe from the production of *The Country Wife* and gave up the entire visit to being photographed against the natural settings.

By now I had opportunities to take photographs of almost anyone I wished to sit for me, and my success as a photographer seemed to help me to be taken more seriously as a designer for the theatre, as a draughtsman, and also as a writer of articles for newspapers and magazines. About this time I had the desire to publish a scrapbook of my photographs, drawings, and articles. My friend Thomas Balston had by now left Messrs. Duckworth, and when I approached several other publishers with the proposal of producing a *"tutti fiori"* of my work, none of them was enthusiastic. Eventually Charles Fry of Batsford, the delightful booksellers and long-established publishers of books on art and architecture in North Audley Street, decided to embark upon the undertaking.

The venture proved successful, and I began a close association with the firm which subsequently published many books of my photographs—*Time Exposure,* with a text by Peter Quennell, *History under Fire,* with James Pope-Hennessy, *Chinese Album, Indian Album,* and travel books written during the war, *Near East* and *Far East.*

Chapter 6 *FASHIONS IN PHOTOGRAPHY AND FASHION PHOTOGRAPHY*

By now I had become established as a photographer, and my photographs were taken for granted. This is one of the disadvantages of being a regular contributor. Admirers of one's work cannot be expected to repeat their eulogies each time it appears, and after a while one feels a certain envy of actors and other creative artists who have direct contact with their audience.

After I felt I had photographed too many people in grottoes of flowers, or against my cotton polka dots, I then began photographing them in a series of baroque settings. As a result of my summer sight-seeing visits in Austria to the churches of Cuvilliés and the brothers Assam, when I arrived in New York the next winter I would comb the trashy antique shops on Third and Madison avenues for carved arabesques or volutes, gesticulating cupids, silver stuccowork, and imitation Tiepolo ceilings. The chaos produced in the studio was like that in the property room of a film studio. Hank Brennan, working in the art department at this time, on hearing complaints about me, said, "He's not really a bad guy. His baroque is worse than his bite."

In general I still used much the same system of light on my sitters as I had aspired to attain in my mother's drawing room; a strong overhead light on the hair, a weak reflected light on the face, and a hot light to give a halo effect at the back of the sitter. The Grand Duchess Marie, who herself was a photographer at this time and knew the technique, reported, "I've just had my picture taken by Cecil Beaton. The portrait came out very regal, but he always sticks a goddamn thousand-watt bulb behind your back to get a halo around the sitter, so I came home with my backside scorched."

I was still somewhat vague about the technical part of the procedure, and we had not yet accustomed ourselves to use light meters for our ex-

*Fashion photograph, showing
studio scene*

*Ruth Ford. An early example of surrealism
in fashion photography.*

posures in the studio, so that a great deal was done by guesswork. When asked by some enthusiastic photographer what lens aperture I used, I was said to have answered, "Oh, I don't know. I just reach around and turn this little brass thing down." Quite a number of plates were ruined by overdevelopment and overexposure; and once when the boy who developed my films tried to help by suggesting I should cut down the exposure, he was severely reprimanded by a rival photographer who also worked in the studio. "Let the bloody fool ruin half his sittings if he wants to." Experts considered that, although my work was "amusing," technically, of course, it "did not exist." Even today, when assistants produce perfect results for me, this criticism is still heard.

The influence of Steichen's work was still paramount in the magazines for which I worked, and some hard binding rules were made by Condé Nast; all the pictures published had to be of the highest standard of technical perfection. However, in spite of my genuine admiration for Steichen's work, I felt that his influence had gone too far when, after an extremely strenuous afternoon's work converting the studio into a luxurious white bedroom (I had mounted a ladder with my camera to photograph Gertrude Lawrence in a bed as light and airy as whipped cream and had remained for one hour on the ladder exposing dozens of plates while Miss Lawrence gave a histrionic performance between the flowered sheets), I was told that the photograph was not considered publishable because in the foreground was a vase of lilies seen out of focus.

When the sittings poured in too thick and fast to give me time for exploration among the junk shops, John Rawlings would act as my property boy and showed great spirit in routing out strange plaster casts, paper or iron objects for me. From the baroque, my backgrounds became more fantastic and were made up of twists of cartridge paper (not lavatory paper, as has been said), sporrans, wire bedsprings, mattresses stood on end, and designs made up of kitchen utensils or gadgets bought at the hardware counter at Woolworth's stores. I enjoyed posing very expensive ladies in these incongruous surroundings, to become part of a pattern of egg beaters, jelly moulds, cutlet frills, or soda-water-bottle containers. It still surprises me that there was never a protest from any of my victims. Later we worked in the studio with large transparent screens of stretched white muslin, which enabled us to indulge in a great variety of shadow effects; and by placing strange objects, and even strange people, on the far side of the screen, we produced a background of fantastic silhouetted shapes.

One afternoon I rushed into the elevator at the Graybar Building, in which the New York Condé Nast office is situated, accompanied by friends and assistants carrying artificial flowers, ostrich feathers made of paper, a plaster cast of a Greek god, hoops of twine, and other strangely assorted objects; I, myself, was carrying seven stuffed white doves. I informed the elevator man that we wanted to go up as soon as possible to the Condé Nast floor. The elevator man looked at me sadly and cracked, "You're telling me!"

Another afternoon a rather timid assistant editor considered that perhaps we were behaving in a somewhat exaggerated manner in the studio and decided to call in Mrs. Chase, the editor in chief, to give her approval of our activities. Mrs. Chase put her head gingerly around the studio door to see Princess Natalie Paley, in a bed of spun glass, being throttled by a young man wearing very little except a heavy design of tattooed roses. Emitting a yelp of alarm, Mrs. Chase fled down the corridors to the comparative sanity of her own office.

One hot summer's day in New York, in order to illustrate an article on "How to Keep Cool," a very peculiar scene was staged in the studio. A number of extremely tough men came up the service elevator wearing medieval-looking gloves and carrying what seemed to be instruments of torture. They hung around asking, "What goes on here?" After an interval the elevator returned, filled to the ceiling with large blocks of ice. At once the medieval torturers set about their business and, using large prongs, started to attack the ice. With enormous skill, but not without a certain percentage of accidents, they proceeded, on my somewhat faltering instructions, to build a wall of ice blocks. Against this wall an ice throne was constructed on which Helen Bennett, the most coveted fashion model at that time, dressed in the minimum of chiffon, sat drinking from a tumbler of lemon juice. When we had the lights organised, the temperature had risen considerably, and a large studio staff was kept busy swabbing with sponges and mops, while Miss Bennett suffered, though by no means in silence.

By this time I had managed to throw off most of my shyness and, gaining self-confidence, developed my range as a photographer. I enjoyed my success, and my days and nights were filled with gaiety and excitement. Each winter I returned to New York to take photographs in which fashion photography played an increasingly important role, and I was blissfully happy working in the well-run studios. The most beautiful models were available, and at my beck and call were a number of assistants who could hurry out at my bidding and come back with statues, trees of azalea or mimosa, gilt pedestals, chandeliers, or butterflies. To the electrical expert I merely had to say, "Let there be light," and there it was. I used the studio's amenities with such gusto that sometimes my assistants would fall from exhaustion; but I went on, myself moving the heavy lights and properties because I could not bear to stop.

During 1935 I wrote in my diary:

After the strenuous physical work done in the studios—and one must be a Hercules to move the lights, the biggest Ionic column, the marble statues, or parts of the backgrounds—I am too wound up with excitement to be able to calm down to anything so peaceful as writing or reading. So I find myself out dancing until two or three each morning.

One afternoon Mrs. Chase came into the studio to watch me take a sitting. At the end she came up to me and said, "Cecil, why do you work so hard? You're only thirty, aren't you? But as I watched you, I noticed you're beginning to look old, and your hair is going grey. Don't work so hard; it isn't worth it." But with the advancing years I work harder and harder. Today I look back on that strenuous period as a comparative holiday.

New Yorkers are always looking for something new, yet often put up great resistance when they first see it. As soon as a fashion has been adopted, one forgets the violence of the impact it produced when it was originally launched. Many times I have met with great opposition to certain photographic trends. But whenever any of my photographs have been greeted with surprise or indignation, I have had a suspicion that my work was good.

One afternoon in 1936 I was about to photograph a number of girls in sports suits, when suddenly I felt I could no longer portray them languishing in the usual attitudes of so-called elegance. I made them put on dark glasses and stand in angular poses with their elbows crooked and their feet planted well apart. Instead of looking like mannequins unconvincingly pretending to be ladies of the *haut monde*, they suggested ballet dancers at rehearsal.

Today it seems odd that these pictures should have created such an uproar in the editorial department of *Vogue*. I was called in for a special conference. What did I mean by making my models looks so unladylike? Was I trying to have a bit of fun at the magazine's expense? I retorted that for me, at any rate, the days of simpering were over. To arch the wrist, raise a little finger like a hook, protect one knee with the other, and pout with raised eyebrows was genteel and ludicrous. In my photographs the models had given up pretence. They were young and fresh and, to my mind, infinitely more alluring; they lent realism to the short sports clothes they showed. So after much deliberation the pictures were allowed to appear, and inaugurated a new phase in the history of fashion photography.

Long before the war had accustomed us to scenes of destruction I decided it might give added piquancy to the artificial smartness of fashion models if, instead of being photographed in drawing rooms, at race courses, or in other suitable surroundings, they were portrayed amid scenes of ruin and destruction. In Paris in 1937 I came across the destroyed and abandoned railway station at Les Invalides. This formed a strange and wonderful background for many of my friends, and my best photographs of Jean Cocteau were taken here.

A few days later I discovered in the Champs Elysées an office building under construction. The workmen had unconsciously created a fantastic décor of cement sacks, mountains of mortar, bricks, and half-finished walls. Mannequins nonchalantly reading newspapers or idling elegantly in this incongruous debris created an extraordinary effect. The results were received with much hesitation by the magazine editors, and instead of being published, as had originally been planned, on six pages, they appeared, somewhat shamefacedly, squashed together on two pages with a trick layout. Nevertheless, even today New York fashion photographers are still searching for corners of desolation and decay, for peeling walls, scabrous billboardings, and rubble to serve as a background for the latest and most expensive dresses.

Some of the more ephemeral fashions in photography have been greeted with justifiable suspicion. The effects of surrealism in fashion were at first alarming. An even more peculiar assortment of properties made its way up the elevators of the Graybar Building to the studio; there were no limits to which we would not go to create a dreamworld.

The fashion photographer, whose importance has only been recognised in the last twenty years, is an extraordinary being. He is generally a painter who could not paint, a designer who never drew, or an architect who never built. He suddenly "found" himself as a photographer. Now he has a curiously undefined yet nevertheless important role in life for which perhaps he considers he is not given enough acclaim. The leading dressmakers of the world are household names, but only those directly concerned with the magazine world have heard of any celebrated fashion photographer. Yet in the world of fashion his role is an influential one. The dressmaker provides the dress, but the photographer must make the woman in that dress appear in a manner that will give all other women a feeling of covetousness. He has to carry on the process of crystallisation from where the dressmaker, the hairdresser, and the jeweller left off. With his taste and perception and his special instinctive sensitivity to the vibrations that are to be picked up simultaneously throughout the world of art and fashion, he must be able to take a model and elevate her into becoming a goddess whom all other women will worship. He must create for her an atmosphere, an entourage,

Surrealism in fashion. This is the picture that caused a furore at its first appearance.

Charles James Coats. 1936.

a niche in the world of fashion. Maybe this niche will be decorated in the Etruscan, Biedermeier, or baroque manner. Maybe it will consist of a grotto of cartridge paper. The fashion photographer's job is to stage an apotheosis.

Sometimes the behind-the-scenes activity is on a fantastic scale. Infinite pains are taken by various experts to assemble the clothes, accessories, jewellery, the backgrounds and properties. There must be necessarily upon the scene a number of lights, electricians to supervise their use, secretaries to attend to various last-minute details, a fashion expert to attend to the arrangement of the clothes and accessories, perhaps a hairdresser, a make-up expert, a jeweller accompanied by a detective, equipped, in case of emergency, with a revolver, and any number of unaccountable bystanders. The psychological situation is always present in the studio, and one participant reacting unfavourably on another may wreck the atmosphere of the sitting. Sometimes, by the time all the details have been taken care of and the photographer is at last able to start his work, the model, who had been subjected to a most elaborate beautifying treatment for many hours previously, has passed endurance point and fainted.

A painter can generally sit down to paint whenever he wishes and need not consider the temperament of half a dozen people. Often it is simply a matter between his model and himself, and sometimes there is no model. Very different is the fashion photographer's task. First he must consider if his model is of a photogenic mould; and in his choice he knows that ordinary, everyday standards do not apply. For instance, if in everyday life a young lady has a slight cast in one eye, it does not necessarily ruin the chances of her being photographed; in fact, a squint has been known to give an added charm. If a model has a head too large for her body, it is almost an advantage, for we do not judge the sitter's head in relation to the body, as we do in everyday life, but the body in relation to the head. The large-headed subject merely looks as if she has an exceptionally tidy little body with small neck, delicate arms and shoulders. In photographs a receding chin looks better than in the flesh; and since one of the greatest difficulties in lighting a face is to organise the nose shadows, for purposes of photography, a nose can hardly ever be too small. Today we have become so accustomed to photographic flattery that unless the photographer has resorted to the base use of wholesale retouching on the negative, and thereby losing the quality of truthfulness in his pictures, we feel the camera has erred on the side of cruelty. We are so accustomed to the over-retouching of second-rate photographers that we seldom believe in the literal accuracy of commercial photographs, and we refuse to admit that the lady holding the toothbrush and smiling can have had any real existence.

Chapter 7 SOME PERSONALITIES

For several winters on end I used to live in New York in a Tower apartment in the Waldorf-Astoria. In my rooms I kept an assortment of photographic lights and equipment, partially hidden behind a screen, so that at any time of day or night I could indulge my photographic passion; sometimes I would be taking pictures until as late as three o'clock in the morning.

At this time Marlene Dietrich became one of my chief sitters. When first she sauntered, in a haze of soft focus, wearing cock's feather and a fishtail skirt, along the corridors of the "Shanghai Express," I was among the most enthusiastic of her millions of spellbound fans, and I longed for the day when I could photograph her. Once, when I happened to be in Paris and, amid great excitement, Miss Dietrich appeared there on holiday, I had tried in vain to waylay her with my camera. I knew from hearsay that she would be game enough to indulge in any fantasy if she once could find time for an appointment; and I evolved in my head many settings in which she would appear as the apotheosis of all the sirens she had thus far created, but it was not until we met in Austria that my ambition was satisfied. The photographic séance was then very different from the one that I had dreamed of.

I met Miss Dietrich the night before she was leaving Salzburg, and when I told her of my photographic longings she suggested I should come to her hotel next morning with my Folding Kodak. I woke excited and early, to discover that, as usual in Salzburg, rain was pouring from the low-hung clouds. When I arrived at her hotel apartment Miss Dietrich was finishing breakfast of coffee and sweet cakes. She wore a silk wrapper, and her face, of a veal-like whiteness, was innocent of *maquillage*. She looked like a German primitive, like a Dürer or a Cranach—completely unlike the moving-picture houri. I considered it might be interesting and unusual to photograph her in this way and begged her not to put on any make-up. She was somewhat surprised, but agreed the experiment might be interesting.

Marlene Dietrich

In Berlin, in the days when Marlene Dietrich was considered a night-club singer of promise, she went one afternoon to be photographed by a Photomaton machine. Quite by accident she discovered that, when photographed in the light of only one lamp placed high above her head, the prominent cheekbones, deep-set eyes, and well-modelled nose were shown to great advantage. Suddenly she realised that a new career was open to her—that of a beauty. From that afternoon on Miss Dietrich saw to it that she was photographed only in a downward light, with the results that the world knows.

But on this rainy morning in Salzburg there was no hope of photographing her in an overhead light. I had no lighting equipment, and as the rain poured down more heavily there was little light of any kind. In an effort to obtain some result I asked Miss Dietrich to crawl on the floor by the window and let me use the breakfast tablecloth as a background. Miss Dietrich yawned, but, as always—for she is the most co-operative of professional models—she complied; she pulled back her hair and gave, in difficult circumstances, an interesting pantomimic performance. Some of the results reminded me of pictures of Duse, but they did not look anything like the Marlene Dietrich her fans had come to admire; they were not beautiful in the conventional glamour manner.

When next time I photographed Miss Dietrich we were in Hollywood, and both the California sun and every type of artificial lighting were available. But, perhaps out of perversity, though I knew how unfailingly successful were all the pictures of her taken in a downward light, I wanted to photograph her in a light unlike that used in all her films and yet make her appear as striking as in everyday existence. When one watched Marlene in any ordinary flat light, she seemed extremely beautiful; and I wanted to prove that she could look beautiful in a hundred different schemes of lighting. Although Miss Dietrich is in the habit of directing the photographer she works with and apparently knows better than anyone how she should be photographed, on this occasion she was willing to put herself entirely in my hands.

In her house in Beverly Hills we photographed for hours, but never once did I place her under the single overhead light. I photographed her in a man's tail coat and top hat, in a clinging garment encrusted with rhinestone embroidery, in feather boas, in cocks' feathers, in every conceivable and inconceivable garment and pose. But when she saw the results she tore them up; they were no good. The face looked unaccountably square and pale; there was no suggestion of the high cheekbones; the eyes had no depth. It had been a long afternoon of failures! At once we took another batch of pictures, and this time Miss Dietrich directed the lighting. Only two lamps were used—one bright one on the hair, which, having a great deal of red in it, looks dark unless very strongly lit, and one high above the camera.

"You'll see! These'll be good!" she said. They were. That afternoon, nearly twenty years ago, I took the pictures of her which are still, to this day, her favourite photographs.

When Miss Dietrich was staying at the Waldorf-Astoria we enjoyed photographic sessions which lasted for many hours and must have broken the record for the longest photographic session there has ever been. We improvised many strange costumes utilising yards of tinsel, orchids, feathers, Merry Widow hats, and spun glass. I pulled her hair into a tight knot on the top of her head, threaded diamond bracelets like a dog collar around her neck, and spent many hours taking pictures in the manner of Boldini portraits, with Marlene making somewhat ambiguous gestures towards a succession of statuettes. The pictures became ever more strange, and my rooms were left looking as if a tornado had swept through them. I know of no other actress who is so enthusiastic in taking up suggestions about new make-ups and general appearance, and many are the times when she has gone to her room on my suggestion that she should alter forthwith the shape of her eyebrows or mouth or hair.

One whole morning was spent photographing Katharine Hepburn, who at this time was enthusiastic at the idea of portraying Joan of Arc on the screen. She had even had her hair cut short in order to accustom herself to the possibility. Miss Hepburn is an excellent photographic subject; her pleasure in posing is only exceeded by the enjoyment of the photographer. At luncheon time we stopped proceedings for a quick sandwich and a glass of milk but soon started again upon another bout of photographs; and Miss Hepburn was still squatting on the sitting-room floor with her head emerging from a tub of full-blown roses when in walked a formidable woman looking somewhat like Mrs. Rittenhouse of the Marx brothers' films. This lady, it was discovered, had made an appointment to be photographed by me, but in my excitement over Miss Hepburn I had entirely forgotten the date.

Miss Hepburn and I went into another room for a secret consultation. Miss Hepburn, it was decided, should wait here while I was photographing Mrs. Rittenhouse, whom i could easily dispose of in a very short session. While Mrs. Rittenhouse was changing from one evening dress to another, she left a coat of silver sequins in my sitting room. Wouldn't that make a wonderful improvised Joan of Arc suit of armour for Miss Hepburn? I crept in to the hidden Miss Hepburn, asked her to put on the coat, and while Mrs. Rittenhouse was being fastened up into a *pervenche* evening dress by my secretary, who had instructions to do the job rather slowly, Miss Hepburn was being photographed as Joan of Arc in Mrs. Rittenhouse's sequins.

Katharine Hepburn

There was a sequel to the Rittenhouse story when I received a letter saying that Mrs. Rittenhouse was much displeased with Mr. Beaton's pictures; that Mr. Beaton had palmed her off with a rushed sitting sandwiched between celebrities.

Two or three winters later I photographed Katharine Hepburn in the more impersonal atmosphere of the studio. Miss Hepburn had previously sent word to enquire if, as she felt she was about to start a cold, she could come to the hotel for the session. Unfortunately this was not possible, and Miss Hepburn, accompanied by her friend, confidante, and secretary, arrived in a mood which struck me as disappointing after the friendliness of our previous encounters. Miss Hepburn did not even thaw into enthusiasm when I showed her the magnificent stuffed peacock I had provided as an appendage for her.

During most of the session she talked earnestly to her friend, who drew closer to my model, so that I found myself focussing in the ground glass onto a well-tailored back. Every picture I took seemed to be an interruption of their heart-to-heart dialogue. At last I asked the friend, perhaps somewhat crisply, if she would mind sitting by the camera. Now I was able to have an uninterrupted view of Miss Hepburn; but as I was surveying her carefully for camera angles in the ground glass, with my head upside down, I saw Miss Hepburn give her friend a broad and unashamed wink. The wink was like a blow between my eyes. I was stunned. How could Miss Hepburn choose this moment, the moment for the closest "scrutiny," for so daring a gesture? There is no abuse calculated to make one feel more impotent or wounded than a wink. Later, however, at dinner in Hollywood, Miss Hepburn, her friend, and I laughed about the incident.

Gloria Swanson is a camera phenomenon. In real life she appears so surprisingly small that one imagines that it would be impossible to present her successfully either in still or in moving pictures. Her neck is short, and her head is out of scale with her diminutive body. But she has the personality and intelligence to turn all disadvantages to advantage. By accentuating the very features that prevent her from becoming a beauty in the classical sense, she becomes beautiful in her own very peculiar way. You feel that she has encouraged her glass-green eyes and her sensitive nose to tilt upwards and her mouth to form a square as, with large, dazzling teeth clenched, she displays her inimitable sneer-smile. She has made of her face something that it is impossible to forget. Nowadays film stars look like each other and also look like anybody. But no one, before or since, has ever looked like Gloria Swanson.

One winter in New York, Gloria Swanson occupied the suite of rooms next to mine in the Waldorf. Our photographic sessions were numerous, and she was such an enthralling subject that it was impossible not to get good results. One can even take a photograph of her when one is drunk. I know; I have succeeded.

Before one of the costume opera balls held at the Metropolitan in New York, Condé Nast was giving a great dinner party in his Park Avenue penthouse. I had for several days been taking *tableaux vivants* pictures of the leading participants of the ball in their elaborate costumes representing figures at the court of Louis Quinze; but it was suggested that I should complete my series on Mr. Nast's terrace after the dinner. I was somewhat averse to this suggestion, as I have always been a little diffident about photographing in full view of an audience. "There's nothing to be alarmed about," I was told. "They're all your friends."

I acquiesced, but I felt unhappy about the whole thing. However, on the terrace we rigged up some elaborate décors of painted pavilions, woodland glades, trellises, bucolic gates, and stuffed sheep. While dressing for dinner in my resplendent finery, disguised as "a gentleman of France," I drank several cocktails; and I drank many more at Mr. Nast's, waiting for the last guests, in their white wigs and silk brocades, to come up in the elevator. At dinner I fortified myself against the session to come by swallowing several glasses of champagne; and when, after the brandy, I went out to the terrace to greet my assistants and give a final nod of approval at the settings for our pictures, I was in a mood of complete serenity.

"Another glass of champagne before you start, sir?"

"Fine! Now then, Madame la Princesse de Talmont! Bring your ostrich-feather fan over here, and sit in profile there on that bench."

Mrs. James Forrestal obliged.

"Now then, Mrs. Schwartz—sorry, the Duchesse de Montbazon—bring your tall plumed hat and come here, please. Where's the Dauphin Louis?"

"Here," and George J. Atwell, Jr., stepped forward.

Between each different batch of sitters who filed past onto the sets I drank a glass of champagne. "Just to sustain you, sir." When I had photographed the entire fancy-dress party I was in no mood to give up.

"Come on! Who else wants to be photographed?" I shouted.

"You've taken everyone in costume—the Marquise de Pompadour, La Reine Catherine, the Duc de Brancas, the whole Polish court group—the whole lot!"

"Oh no! We must take some more pictures! Yes, I'll have another glass, thank you."

"Well, there are only a few people who've come up to have a look-see. They're not in costume."

"Doesn't matter!"

I photographed Condé Nast in his tail coat, sitting with Mrs. Chase, surrounded by sheep. Likewise I photographed Mr. and Mrs. Harrison Williams. Each picture called for a celebration libation. By now I could hardly focus in the ground glass of the camera. I started to giggle.

"But this is the way photographs should *always* be taken!" I decided, wielding a glass of champagne. "Hullo, Gloria! What are you doing here?" I had spied Gloria Swanson standing quizzically in the doorway wearing a wonderful evening dress of taffeta made of every sort of purple, mauve, and magenta. "Why aren't you dressed up?" I asked her somewhat euphemistically.

"I just came to have a look-see."

"Come and be photographed!"

The pictures I took of Gloria Swanson that night were better than many others I took at other long sessions during the many years we have worked together.

Mrs. Patrick Campbell stands out in my memory above all others I photographed one New York winter. I had but recently met this already legendary figure and was impressed by the quality of greatness which she exuded. I was flattered that Mrs. Pat seemed to like me, and I nurtured our new acquaintance in many ways, even going for elocution lessons to her overheated room in the unpretentious hotel where she then lived. It was Mrs. Pat's triumph that, although almost penniless, her sense of beauty and poetry overcame all poverty and the disadvantages of age. When after much hesitation she consented to be photographed by me, I was fully aware of how momentous was the occasion.

Mrs. Pat came into the studio dressed like the traditional stage duchess. She wore a black velvet dress with a small hat, which she had bullied the manageress of some shop into giving her on the strength of today's sitting, a great row of artificial pearls, and she brought with her her dog Moonbeam. It was her love for this white Pekinese that prevented Mrs. Pat from accepting invitations to return to the London stage; she refused to expose Moonbeam to the necessary six months of quarantine.

As soon as Mrs. Pat appeared my assistants Jack and Jimmie perked up; their eyes showed an interest seldom aroused in them by the usual sitters. They were soon an enraptured audience, and Mrs. Pat gave a wonderful performance. She mooed like a cow, bellowed, threw her hands to the skies, and went off into peals of deep cavernous laughter. She sat on a garden seat which I had provided—a mess of crushed black velvet, pearls, and fur. She bathed in her old fur coat.

Mrs. Patrick Campbell

"Isn't it a beauty? I've worn it for six years. It was left me by my greatest woman friend, Brigit Guiness, and she wore it for six years, and it's just as warm and comfortable and luxurious as ever it was. It's flying squirrel. You see, you blow it and the fur is soft and blue-grey all the way down. It hasn't been dyed, and it wears so well. I wrap myself in it, and I'm as comfortable as in a house. But oh how terrible that you photograph me as I am now. Why didn't you appear forty years ago? I was a beauty then. You could have taken wonderful pictures then. But now what can you do with all these dewlaps? I look like an old paper bag which has burst. Oh, why can't I be a beauty?" she wailed, to the accompaniment of laughter from Jack and Jimmie.

Once the photography started, Mrs. Pat could not remain serious for long. She would pose so that her profile was exhibited to the gods, and we, poor mortals, could but catch a glimpse of her underchin. Then, after moaning about the horrors of old age, her eyes would twinkle and again she would explode with laughter.

A few days after I had sent her the proofs of the pictures Mrs. Pat came to tea to show me which she preferred. Along with my proofs she also brought a selection of pictures which had been taken when she played Mélisande and Paula Tanqueray. These documents showed a magnolia beauty with raven hair and dark pools for eyes, and it was almost alarming to compare them with her now and to witness the transformation of that exquisite, mysterious-looking creature. Although Mrs. Pat still possessed a majestic quality and an innate grandeur, it must be conceded that she had become a fat old woman with few relics of past beauty.

"Look at the glory of that neck, at that line of cheek, and look at me now, sagging like an old cow! Look at that jaw, and now look at me! All wind and water. Oh God! How can He be so unkind to do this to me? Why must we suffer this terrible change? Why must we all become ugly? I don't know how some women stand it. I don't know how they don't commit suicide!" And then her eyes would twinkle and her pursed lips quiver into a raucous Hogarthian laugh.

By merely discussing the rather ordinary pictures I had taken of her, she distilled some magic into them. "No one has taken such a photograph of gloves! Those hands are not dead like most hands in gloves! These gloves are alive! Look at the beauty, the depth between the thumb and first finger! That's what everyone wants to have! And look at that shadow under the jaw! Oh, it's so useful! So flattering and so *clever!* Oh! You're a genius to put in that shadow!"

And she rhapsodised about the beauty of her dog Moonbeam. "You can understand my giving up a career for a dog with eyes like that, can't you?

You can realise why I couldn't go back to England and let that little dog die?" She started to fumble in the depths of a black velvet bag. "Now, I've brought you forty dollars for these pictures."

I protested and said I had no intention of letting her buy any of the photographs; they were meant as a tribute from an admirer. But eventually she said it was rather affected of me to "carry on like this" and she insisted upon giving me thirty dollars which she could well afford, as she now had a rich pupil, and I'd worked so hard and made a work of art out of a pair of gloves which Gladys Cooper had bought for her at Bloomingdale's.

Mrs. Pat did everything with a certain grandeur. When she was writing this cheque, a dollar became for me—perhaps for the first time—something as beautiful and worthy of respect as a golden coin; all the vulgarity and stigma associated with the word disappeared. "I've brought you forty dollars" sounded like the beginning of a beautiful speech. Mrs. Pat told me she was poor, but, she explained, "I'm not ashamed of being poor, and I am accustomed to it. I could easily have been rich if I'd been just a little bit vulgar or broken a little dog's heart."

During the thirties the lady who became the Duchess of Windsor was one of my most frequent subjects. Among the rewards of a photographic career is the intimacy that sometimes springs up between the photographer and those who sit for him; and after the first occasion on which I had spent a six-hour session with Mrs. Simpson, at the time of her rumoured engagement to the Prince of Wales, I felt I knew her almost as well as some of my close friends. After some time I had been amazed to find myself asking her a number of questions to which a large proportion of mankind was, at this very time, so anxious to know the answers; and, strangely enough, Mrs. Simpson did not appear to resent the intimacy which the camera had helped to create between us. Mrs. Simpson was, from the earliest time I photographed her, dressed always with the trim silhouette of a Chinese figurine, but she was, nevertheless, a far from easy subject, though she has grown considerably more photogenic since she became the Duchess of Windsor.

In an American wisecracking idiom she is extremely entertaining; she treated the question of photography with the businesslike thoroughness that is typical of her. But when first I photographed her I did not know how to show her to her best advantage and had trouble, for instance, in posing her extremely utilitarian-looking hands; she herself gave me little help. Today the hands have acquired a clever way of finding an unobtrusive position in the composition of any photograph, and she realises that the most successful pictures of herself are those which show the sparkle of amusement in the eyes and the varieties of expression that run across her very vital face.

The Duchess of Windsor

The Duke of Windsor

The Duke and Duchess of Windsor on their wedding day

In May 1937, a short time before her marriage to the Duke of Windsor, at the time when she was the cynosure of half the world, I visited her in order to take some official photographs in the Château de Candé, where she was staying as the guest of the now deceased Charles Bédeaux. There had been so many unflattering snapshots of her in the press that she felt perhaps it was now time to be seen by the world in a more appealing guise. In contrast to the pictures taken in clothes of a smartly modernistic aspect, I suggested making romantic-looking pictures in dresses which were less of the moment but more softly becoming in line than the currently fashionable tubular skirts and square-shouldered jackets. Billowing dresses were produced; pictures were taken in the shade of sunlit trees with thick grass covered with daisies, and a greyhound which appeared unexpectedly made a useful accompaniment. Even the rather hideous Château de Candé proved a good background. Mrs. Simpson, though somewhat afraid of having to tread in the long grass—for her dog Slippers had recently died after being bitten by a viper—entered into the spirit of the occasion with courage and joked about the discomforts of walking in evening frocks through the oil of the garages which we passed on our way to the more sylvan scenes in the park.

At least a hundred pictures were taken, and the results of this sitting created a stir when Condé Nast decided to devote eight pages to their presentation in the American edition of *Vogue*. They were flashed on the screens as "stills" in the movie palaces in America, and although a certain amount of criticism was directed at the over-life-size lobster which decorated the skirt of one of the dresses, so spectacularly successful had the results of the photographs been that in June I was asked to return to the château to take photographs of the wedding. At first I felt that my trip to Touraine was somewhat redundant; but I am glad that I was able to be at the château at this time, for I was received with the greatest cordiality and affection by the bridal pair, and although my pictures were taken the day before the marriage, I felt I was present at the scene of one of the strangest human dramas in modern English history. Here is a description I wrote at the time:

At Tours Station a row of photographers waited to snap anyone who had anything whatsoever to do with the wedding. Mrs. Simpson's hairdresser was photographed; so was her photographer, but the result appeared in the French papers with the caption, *"Le curé arrive pour les noces."*

Outside the château gates a litter of journalists, their vans and motorcycles; inside on the lawns, swans and dogs looked very peaceful. Mrs. Spry and Miss Pirie (of "Flower Decorations") with large trailing branches of blossoms were calmly decorating the château with mountains of mixed flowers. Only the gleam in the footman's eyes denoted that excitement was in the air. Just as I was about to make my arrangements for taking pictures, a car drove up and caused great consternation and activity, for it contained the clergyman who, out of the blue, and at the eleventh hour, had volunteered to marry the Duke of Windsor to Mrs. Simpson.

The Rev. Robert Jardine proved to be a comic-looking little man with a red bun face, protruding teeth, and a broad grin. Wallis was anxious to complete the arrangements with the clergyman before devoting herself to photography, and the Duke walked in the garden with him back and forth for so long, and seemed to be in such deep consultation, that I worried lest our photography should never start. But the clergyman needed much attention, of course; he wanted an altar. Well, what could be used as an altar? The entire household, Bédeaux, Rogers, the Metcalfes, the Duke, Wallis, and myself, ran from room to room looking for a suitable piece of furniture. The table with the lamp on it? No . . . The table with the drinks on it? Too square. This other one? Too low. What about the chest from the hall? A heavily carved Renaissance chest showed a row of overfat caryatides proffering a richly embossed slab. The Duke, in great spirits, like a small boy home for the holidays, exclaimed, "Marvellous. That's marvellous; couldn't be better. But put it farther back; put it here . . . there . . . no, a little more this way." He directed the movements of the chest by cupping his hands and flapping the fingers to and fro, then, completely lacking in self-consciousness, he got down on hands and knees to tuck in the carpet under the altar and to measure the distance each side of the altar to the wall. The measurement slide would break. "These damned things always break," he said as he pocketed the remains. "And now for a cloth for the altar." What could be used? Wallis, pointing to the caryatides, said, "Oh yes. We must have something to cover up that row of 'extra' women! We can't let them bulge through a thin cloth. We must have a proper cloth."

"If only I'd brought some of my photographic background materials," I ejaculated. "They're tinselly, and some even look like brocade."

"Oh, I've got a tea cloth," says Wallis.

"Yes, the one we bought in Budapest," says the Duke.

The tea cloth is produced from the bottom of the linen trunk already packed for the honeymoon. It is a pretty cloth—pale coffee-coloured with silver-thread leaves in it—exceedingly fine and delicate and almost suitable for an altar cloth. But Wallis's Cockney maid is furious at having to unpack the trunk and whines, "If it's as much trouble as this getting married, I'm sure I'll never go through with it myself!" Wallis later explained, "I couldn't let the poor girl be put off matrimony for life. I felt it my bounden duty to say, 'Oh, it's not always as bad as this, but it just happens to be if you're marrying the ex-King of England.'"

The altar cloth fixed, Mr. Allen, with a rather defiant expression on his face, brought in two large candlesticks to place on the altar. The Duke praised the effect. "That looks fine." But Wallis cracked, "Hey, you can't put those there now. We want them for the dinner table tonight."

Mrs. Spry and accomplice continued to drag in more and more flowers from the conservatory, where huge pink and white peonies bulged over their troughs, cascades of lilies, syringa, acanthus, and flowering laurel lay on sheets, and spikes of white yucca rose from the drinking buckets. The flowers were out of all proportion to the scale of the house and the small numbers of people who would see them, and Mrs. Spry was being so conscientious about their arrangement that several times she would redo an enormous monument of mixed flowers with which she was not entirely pleased. This extravagance of Wallis is typical, and, on second thoughts, I realised that she had done well. She knew the setting of the château, with its pretentious and rather bad furniture, would be somewhat overwhelmed by this floral welter, and now the general effect was certainly gay and festive.

The small music room, where the marriage was to be performed, was more or less ready. Should the window curtains behind the altar be drawn or not? It was a pity the window was off centre. No matter how much measuring the Duke did with his foot rule, the window would always be cockeyed; no matter what readjustments were made, the room would look like a rather ordinary little drawing room with sickly pea-green walls on which hung French engravings (over the altar the subject framed was "The Crowning of Voltaire on the Stage of the Comédie Française"), while a bad oil portrait of Madame Bédeaux took pride of place. A row of crushed-strawberry-coloured chairs had been carefully arranged by Wallis and the Duke, but after all their diligence the "placement" was many times negligently disarranged by servants and others who had to pass through the room.

I stood about looking into my camera, wondering where on earth I could best get impressive photographs. It was sad for anyone who had mental visions of Westminster Abbey to hear the Duke say, "That's marvellous—and looks just like a church." But at any rate the clergyman was gratified and said that now the photographs might start.

Maurice, my French assistant, and the electricians had fixed up the lights in a bedroom upstairs, and we began by taking pictures of the Duke alone. The Duke will never allow the right side of his face to be photographed and likes the parting of his hair to be shown, and so firm was he on this point that he had the postage stamp on which his profile was shown redesigned accordingly, but otherwise he was very pliable and easy to pose, and he tried his hardest to make it less difficult for me by showing great vitality and keenness. He approved of sitting on a cushioned stool, because it was different from the usual chair; he did not wish to be smoking a cigarette. His expression, though intent, was essentially sad; the tragic eyes, fiercely blue, and one a fraction lower in the face than the other, belied the impertinent tilt of the nose. At forty-three years old his hair is as golden and thick as a youth's of sixteen; although he looked somewhat wrinkled, he was essentially young and schoolboyish. Whether or not he will be pleased with my photographs I cannot tell, for they will not be flattering to him, and he is accustomed to seeing only the highly retouched pictures taken of himself as Prince of Wales many years ago.

In spite of constant interruptions, I was quite content with the pictures I took under trying conditions. While the Duke was on the telephone to the British Embassy in Paris, endeavouring to find a crucifix to put on the improvised altar, Wallis, now in a black dress with huge pear-diamond clips, was waiting to be photographed with her husband-to-be. Eventually the bridal couple sat hip to hip on a huge pouf, the Duke's hand around Wallis's waist. The background was a difficulty, and over a screen—partly as a joke which I could not resist—I threw a beautifully needle-worked counterpane of pink satin.

An interval for luncheon before taking the pictures in the wedding clothes. The Duke, who seldom eats anything in the middle of the day, today had a plate of strawberries and cream. But the others ate a delicious meal, and there were funny stories to be told of the morning's work—of someone painting all the travelling labels red by mistake—how there were 500 letters for the Duke, 300 for Wallis, and telegrams arriving every moment.

Now the Duke must change into his wedding clothes for the photographs. Wallis did not like the chosen shirt or waistcoat. "But it must be a light waistcoat, mustn't it? And I've got a nice white shirt, but I don't want that to be crumpled for tomorrow, and this won't show. But I must have a carnation—a white carnation. Isn't that the conventional thing for the bridegroom to have?" Upstairs hung Wallis's "Wallis-blue" wedding dress and, on a stand by the window, a bonnet of pale blue feathers with a tulle halo effect.

The Duke came in and caught a glimpse of his bride in her wedding dress. "Oh! So this is the great dress! Well, it's lovely! Very pretty!"

He still speculated about a buttonhole. I picked a small cluster of Mrs. Sinkins pinks from a vase to make a synthetic carnation, but the Cockney maid, now recovered from her morning's tantrums, produced an imitation carnation of her own.

In case sight-seers or photographers with telescopic lenses should catch a sight of the betrothed couple, we had to confine our activities to certain screened parts of the château and its garden. The sun poured down, and the steps of the terraces made an excellent setting. But as they posed with their heads so close to one another I could not help feeling that they made an incongruous pair. As the lady at the ribbon counter would say, their faces do not "go" together; they "swear." The Duke, so blond and insouciant, exudes an aura of tweed, Scotty dogs, and briar pipes, an essentially "outdoor" type; she, so polished and sophisticated, with her sleek dark hair, belongs to the world of restaurants and drawing rooms. At one point Dudley Forwood, the equerry, brought some disturbing news to the Duke, whose face suddenly became quite tragic. Wallis, too, looked harassed, and for some minutes it was impossible for me to say, "Please both look pleasant." Eventually Wallis said, "Anyhow, let's remember we're having our pictures taken," and the sitting continued.

We took pictures in front of the improvised altar by the floral decorations. I took pictures of the Duke with Carter, the Duke's detective, and the mail trays which were piled high with letters all bearing the Duke's profile. At last there was no excuse to take any more photographs. Before changing their wedding clothes the bridal couple posed for a few seconds for an old friend of the Duke's who had worked for many years at a somewhat old-fashioned firm of court photographers. He was, it was explained, a nice reliable photographer—maybe a bit conventional—for, of all the rooms in the château, had he not elected to photograph in the darkest and most ornate of all?

The photographer, a delightful man with grey hair, came up to me and presented his card, saying, "I see no reason why there should be rivalry or enmity between photographers." I felt supercilious and a little patronising. Later I had reason to think differently.

"Aunt Bessie" Merryman presided over the tea and appended the addresses to the telegrams which had arrived from Baltimore, while Wallis opened the latest batch of letters, some personal, some anonymous—one she showed me enclosed a cutting with "Disgusting" written across it. She explained she opened all her letters herself, as she insisted on feeling the pulse of the country.

It was now time for me to leave. That evening in Paris I saw my pictures freshly developed. I was approached by photographic agents who informed me, "The *Queen Mary* sails tonight; if your pictures could be sent now, they would arrive in the U.S. one whole week before the general press pictures could possibly get there, so your prints are worth an enormous sum." (This, of course, was before photographs were flown across the Atlantic.) One American agent informed me that fifteen hundred pounds had been paid for the Coronation pictures, but added, "These are of more interest. It is the greatest human-interest story of the age." But my *Vogue* obligations prevented me from thus capitalising on the pictures, and when I returned to London several hours before the wedding ceremony had taken place at the Château de Candé, and the press of the world had not been admitted past the château gates, I discovered that the picture taken by the "old-fashioned photographer" had already been reproduced in the *Evening Standard*, radioed to America, and that duplicate prints were already on their way aboard the *Queen Mary*.

Of all the photographic illustrations I have ever made for books or articles, none has afforded me as much hilarious entertainment as the series, taken in imitation of the work of Victorian and Edwardian court photographers, for my book of burlesque memoirs entitled *My Royal Past*. In fact, no other work upon which I have ever embarked has been so lighthearted from beginning to end. When the book appeared, many people remarked upon the enormous amount of settings and the tremendous period wardrobe we must have acquired to provide so many elaborate plates. I must now confess that a number of pictures of the Grand Duchess and her lady in waiting, Countess

Bülop, were photomontages, and that I spent many congenial weeks pasting different-sized faces of Tilly Losch and Don Antonio Gandarillas onto old illustrations cut out from *Figaro* and *La Mode*. But in order to give an effect of verisimilitude, a large number of pictures had to be taken for this especial purpose. I corralled some of my friends to appear as characters from the life story: they entered conscientiously into the spirit of the period and spent much time acquiring the wigs, costumes, jewellery, or uniforms. An expert gave me all information about the correct procedure regarding the wearing of orders and decorations, and infinite care and precision were taken that the picture should appear quite authentic. For weeks on end I called on my leading players, Tilly Losch, Antonio Gandarillas, Frederick Ashton, Sir Francis Rose, and Christian Bérard, to appear in new situations I had evolved for them.

One summer afternoon I had planned, with several of my dramatis personae, an elaborate expedition to Windsor, where, at Clewer Park, an old lady named Mrs. Mosscockle lived in Edwardian splendour. Mrs. Mosscockle (née Rita Sparrow), with pillar-box painted cheeks and a turquoise-blue toque perched on a cake of marmalade-coloured hair, boasted that when she drove through the streets of Windsor in her open carriage Eton boys still took off their top hats to her and bowed, in the belief that she was the re-incarnation of Queen Alexandra. Mrs. Mosscockle's house was as untouched by changing fashions of decoration as her clothes; the drawing-room blinds were drawn during the hours of daylight lest the flowered carpets should lose their ruby brilliance. Enormous pots of oriental china were filled with pampas grass. Each room possessed dozens of small tables, all covered with serried rows of small photographs in gilt and silver frames. Clewer Park, in every detail, was an ideal background for illustrations for my book, and Mrs. Mosscockle had graciously consented, not only to give me the hospitality of her house for an afternoon, but herself to pose.

With several laundry baskets, filled with court uniforms and ball dresses, strapped onto the backs of five motors, we set off. No sooner had we started on our journey than a streak of lightning almost blinded us, a thunderclap reverberated against the drums of our ears, and the windscreens of the motors became a running torrent of hot summer rain. The sky was black, the roads soon flooded, panic was in the air, and a coalman's cart horse bolted in terror. We drove forward at a few miles an hour into an ever-darker abyss. I realised that in such lack of daylight any indoor photography would be impossible, for, since the early photographs I was about to emulate were taken in daylight, I had not brought electric lights with me. We must alter our plans.

Walter Sickert and his wife at Bath. 1942.

Nicholas Nabokov

Salvador Dali. 1936.

Merle Oberon

Aldous Huxley

Lord David Cecil

Laurence Olivier

Only a few days before, I had visited the studio of Thomas Downey, the Edwardian photographer, whose business was now being carried on by an elderly white-haired lady in Ebury Street. I had been enthralled by the collection of rare photographs from the past which she had shown me, and I was overjoyed to find that many of the original backgrounds and properties were still in existence in her studio. Instead of continuing through the deluge to Windsor, suddenly the five motors stopped, turned about, and drove through the tropical torrent to the studio in Ebury Street. I explained to the old lady that I wished to hire her studio for the afternoon and would like her to help me with the photography. At first she looked aghast at such a sudden and overwhelming invasion of her premises, and for several minutes continued to appear rather worried, but as business was bad at the time—I doubt if she had had any sitters for years past—she resigned herself to becoming part of the afternoon's eccentricity.

The laundry baskets were brought in sopping from the tropical storm, which continued all afternoon to give a melodramatic background to our activities. We telephoned our regrets to Mrs. Mosscockle and started to unpack. Suddenly the Downey Studio came to life again with tiaras, diamond stars, orders, swords, white kid gloves, furs, and ermine-trimmed trains. The old lady had some misgiving about the wisdom of allowing me the hospitality of her studio when Sir Francis Rose, with his large walrus moustache, proceeded to don an apricot-coloured brocade dress and a huge picture hat decked with Maréchal Niel roses; and when the Countess von Bülop appeared in full court splendour, she was no longer convinced that she had done right to entertain us. Nevertheless, I was able to reassure her, and she soon set about helping me with the old-fashioned backgrounds, lights, and camera.

When my subjects first posed before the lens that afternoon I was so convulsed with laughter that tears coursed down my cheeks. The elderly lady looked at me with renewed suspicion. But as the afternoon progressed she entirely entered into the mood of the occasion and would trip forward to alter the line of a court train or place a protruding toe at the correct angle. After an orgy of royal photography we even induced the lady herself to be dressed up in some of our clothes, and, wearing a blue-and-white brocade dress and a tiara on her white tresses piled high, she glowers into the camera and appears vignetted in the book as "My Wonderful Mother."

Chapter 8 WAR EXPERIENCES

A s THE years passed pleasantly by I was contented with the way I lived; but, even so, I would receive an occasional jolt when it occurred to me how large a proportion of my life had already been spent merely in taking photographs. I felt no inclination to abandon photography altogether, yet I was convinced in five years' time I would certainly not be a photographer. More than two decades had passed since the day of my first exhibition, and I had signed contracts for a further period of photographic work. I wondered if I had really developed as an artist, or whether I had merely commercialized my talent. I decided to develop other media and, with the greatest difficulty, applied myself to writing.

Then the war came. It was decided that I could only be of any use as a photographer, and it was as a photographer that I lived till 1945.

During the early phases of the war I worked in London for the Ministry of Information. At first I tried to do something interesting photographically that might be more effective than the conventional recruiting and propaganda posters. But although I had a number of sittings, the results, by the time they had been approved by various committees, cut up and rearranged by various art departments, were so unlike my work, and so like all other posters, that I felt discouraged. Then I concentrated on photographing the current war leaders. The telephone pealed constantly with secretaries making appointments; Lord Halifax was dated up for three o'clock at the Foreign Office, General Ironside at six at the War Office, and Sir John Simon at ten next morning at the Treasury, to be followed by Sir Cyril Newall at the Air Ministry at noon.

Here was a field of activity to which I was entirely unaccustomed. I was full of trepidation. Although my new sitters showed consideration for my job, few of them had ever heard of me; and it was an interesting experience to be treated as an ordinary press photographer. But I found that my previous experience now stood me in good stead. I was able to bring out many of my familiar tricks and also discovered how easy, in comparison to photographing beautiful women of the world, it is to photograph men. The "photographer of men" has chosen an easy life.

Here are a few diary extracts I wrote:

At the War Office the Chief of Staff was busy. The A.D.C. confided that the general had cancelled his afternoon ride and that any moment a meeting might be called. From the tone of awe I detected in the A.D.C.'s voice, I felt perhaps he meant to indicate that any time now an offensive might be embarked upon. My imagination took wing. So the "phony" war was about to end! I felt quite sick with trepidation. Outside in a London drizzle, the grey domes and towers of Whitehall looked quiet and peaceful, remote from this sinister room with its "secret" telephones, "secret" communications, "secret" despatch cases, and the drawers marked "Western Front," "Palestine," and "Balkans."

When I went into the Chief's study, General Ironside was writing in his diary. A giant, seven foot tall, a soldier of the old school, rugged, leonine, with piercing blue eyes, reliable, honest, he sat smoking his pipe and continued to write at his desk while my electricians plugged in their lights.

The general wrote page after page in a rather schoolboyish longhand. I was unwilling to disturb him until the last necessary moment. I fished around the island of his desk to find good angles for my photographic catches. "We'll start here," I whispered to the assistants, and trained my camera on him. Gradually, while focussing in the ground glass, I realised that, no longer upside down, I could read every word of the great schoolboy's diary.

Another sitter was the Minister of Labour. Ernest Bevin good-humouredly resented my photographing him against the grand staircase of the Ministry of Labour. "You're trying to make me look more Royalist than the King! I suppose you think America expects me to have the Duke of Buccleuch's background."

In some lights Mr. Bevin looks coarse and malevolent; in others, Hogarthian and benign; in some, strong and impressively healthy.

"I'll go on standing here if you really want me to," he said, "but, you know, we've got to win this war, and I've got to get on with the job."

A group of minions surrounded him, pipes in their mouths and hands in pockets. I noted how different their behaviour was from that of Lord Halifax's underlings at the Foreign Office who showed such respect for their Minister. Here was a circle of confederates. A rumbling joke was started; the laughter increased and became an avalanche; it was comforting, at this disastrous moment in our nation's history, to hear such laughter.

As I bid good-bye, Mr. Bevin was in the middle of another bout of amusement;

tears were pouring out of his eyes as he waved his fat hand hopelessly in the centre of further guffaws.

On the morning of the Simon sitting I was in the Board Room at the Treasury in good time to listen to the electricians' lugubrious suggestions for overcoming the always unexpected snags which befall them. The noble room by Kent, with magnificent furniture and a gallery of portraits and marble busts of former Chancellors of the Exchequer, was a propitious setting. The entrance of the Chancellor was dramatically contrived. While I awaited Sir John, various secretaries told me that the Chancellor enjoyed being photographed, would give a great deal of time to it, and be amenable in every possible way. We waited. A telephone call was put through to the Chancellor's home to know why he was late. Is this he coming now? Expectations were high. No. An anticlimax. More cursory talk. More looking at wrist watches. I believe I hear him. Is it he? Yes! Sir John appeared. Tall, handsome, white-haired, with a sheaf of papers under his arm, he boomed, "Good morning, gentlemen," as he walked, an upright figure, boldly to his desk. Here he became suddenly a little crabbed and crotchety.

"Why have you turned my wife's picture away from me?" I had turned the picture so that it would show in the photograph I was about to take.

"Where is the silver inkstand? One of the things of beauty in this room."

A minion hesitantly explained that the inkstand had been taken down to the cellars at the beginning of the war for safety, as it was also a thing of value. Another inkstand—a later copy of the missing one—was brought in after a short interval.

Sir John rearranged several objects on his desk. Eventually he was ready to pose. Yes, the secretaries were right. Sir John did seem to enjoy being photographed. His attitude reminded me of a certain schoolmaster at my private school at Eastbourne, and I was pleased to include, in a prominent position on Sir John's desk, two bottles of acid drops. We moved around the room, and I asked Sir John to remain stationary for a moment near a bust of Pitt.

"No," said the Chancellor, "that is not a good idea; the bust is too big."

"Well, will you move along to the centre of that giant mahogany table—the Board Room Treasure, as I am told—so as to be flanked by a smaller bust of Pitt and one of Disraeli?"

The Chancellor turned his head. "I don't think that's a good idea either. Disraeli was a very poor Chancellor. I don't wish to be photographed with him; it is pointless."

"Then perhaps over here by the fireplace?"

"That's an entirely different idea. That's Robert Peel, one of the greatest, *the* greatest Chancellor, England has ever known." And smilingly, Sir John posed by the bust in various lighting arrangements until I had had really more than enough.

Anthony Eden

Lord Halifax

Winston Churchill

"Well, that is the end of the session for today, sir." I bowed.

"Have you finished your dose?" the Chancellor asked, looking somewhat disappointed. "Well, if you've done with me, er—well—er, I'll be going, as," with sudden modesty he confessed, "I *have* got a few things to do."

I also photographed Sir Kingsley Wood (whose powers of concentration enabled him to digest the contents of the scarlet leather boxes while a dozen men were talking in his room), Anthony Eden, Sir John Anderson (whose newly married wife moaned, on seeing the results, "Oh, oh, oh! You've cut off his moles!"), and many who had the highest offices and on whom vast responsibilities lay, but whose names are already only dimly remembered.

The war had reached one of its grimmest periods when I was summoned to photograph its staunch leader, Winston Churchill. For the last six weeks England had been bombed almost continually, and we were now expecting an invasion. Here are the notes I made in my diary:

I awoke to a cold grey morning. For two months now no gas or hot bath, so shaved in a little pot of warm water and was late in starting off. In the stress of getting from one part of London to another in time for my next appointment, I often forget the address, so that the taxi driver waits while I ring various door-bells in vain. Today, however, no such difficulty. No. 10 Downing Street is not an address one could forget.

When I arrived at No. 10 they were all rather feverish. Mrs. Hill, Mr. Church-ill's secretary, said that she had tried to call me to come earlier, but my telephone was always busy. The Prime Minister was already in the Cabinet Room and would not allow lights to be rigged up while he was working there. Somewhere else? I raced from room to room, followed by electricians. As usual, time was short, and lights take so long to instal. We hurried through three living-reception rooms giving on to a pretty little passage which Sir Philip Sassoon imaginatively turned into a small dining room where Mr. and Mrs. Churchill dine alone, the big parties taking place in the imposing and hideously panelled dining hall next door, with its tenth-century pottery, enormous Greek urns, and fine Victorian silver dishes.

I was taken to Mrs. Churchill, who was downstairs in a reinforced basement room.

"You must come and see Winston right away," she said, smiling. "Is the Prime Minister in there?" she fluttered to a secretary.

Somehow I was unable to say that I was not yet ready for a visit to the great man, that it would be better to delay until camera and lights were prepared. However, I had missed the opportunity. Further doors leading to Adam-deco-rated rooms were opened, and from the final secretary's room I was able to catch the first glimpse of my goal. Through a double door, heavily lined, past a couple of Corinthian columns, at the centre of an immensely long table sat the Prime Minister, heavy, immaculate, with pink wax complexion. A vast cigar was freshly affixed in his mouth. Plump white tapering fingers were deftly turning through the papers in a red leather box at his side; the interruption of a visit was obviously displeasing. "You know Mr. Beaton, don't you? He's come to take a photograph of you," said Mrs. Churchill.

This announcement, at the busiest moment of the morning, was not likely to be welcome. The Prime Minister grumbled gruffly, "Ah, yes. I've heard you're very clever," and then inarticulately huh-huhed. I stood like a village wight, not knowing how to proceed. Certainly I was at a disadvantage in not having my paraphernalia ready; but luckily I had a trump card and threw down before the great man the first photographs, just rushed through from the developer, of his grandson, Winston Churchill, Jr. The atmosphere lightened; but I soon retreated, leaving the Prime Minister to his work, and appealed to his competent secretaries to help me as soon as possible to arrange lights in a reception room.

Meanwhile Mrs. Churchill very kindly showed me the rooms upstairs. Her own bedroom was charming with chintz flowers and as pretty as any bedroom in the country. Indeed, I was impressed by the fact that all the bedrooms and corridors which give shelter to our most important figures in the land look like part of a small country house. The Prime Minister's bedroom could not have been more simple; a small single bed, a washbasin with shaving soap and brushes in evidence, only a few books, some files of Parliamentary speeches, on the wall a drawing of his mother, a bedside table mounted with many telephones and boxes of cigars, and that was all—except for the wonderful and ornate view from the windows out to the Horse Guards Parade and the Admiralty.

Mrs. Churchill pointed out a carfull of pigeons below. "Those are being trained in case all else fails. They are pigeons to send with last-minute messages. Once more we revert to the primitive," she said.

Then a secretary summoned Mrs. Churchill, and another summoned me. "You must hurry, for the P.M. has an eleven o'clock appointment," reiterated the secretary.

The electricians had tried to fix up the big camera and lights in the reception room, but the lights would not go on, and the devil was in my own assistant today. Everything he did went wrong, and he was incapable of getting started; he suffered as much as I. There are days like this when the wires are never long enough and it seems that nothing will ever be ready. We fixed up a somewhat inadequate arrangement against a yellow marble column in an empty room, and then I hurried downstairs to await our fate with a small camera and some flash bulbs.

We were told that the Prime Minister must leave any minute now. It was already ten minutes to eleven. Secretaries passed by the hall and were cheerful and busy. I was nervous and made stilted conversation about the sitting-to-come with my assistant. The butler passed by with a glass of port on a silver tray.

At eleven o'clock came a great whispering that the Prime Minister had just started to dictate to his secretary, Mrs. Hill. The Whip, David Margesson, appeared and talked about recent air-raid damage. Other secretaries crossed and recrossed the hall several times. No word from the Holy of Holies. Ten past eleven; a quarter past eleven; twenty past eleven. Some more servants of the government appeared. The Prime Minister had had to change the eleven o'clock appointment, but it was absolutely necessary for him to leave at eleven twenty-five—he had a Cabinet appointment at eleven-thirty. Mrs. Hill, white and worried, put her head round the door. "Would you just take a few pictures in here now? There is no time to go upstairs."

We went into the Cabinet Room. The long desk was partly covered with stationery, the windows blocked here and there with brown paper improvisations where the panes had been blasted. Not much light, but no moment to be lost. I clicked from a far vantage point, and my assistant let off a flash. I imagine perhaps the Prime Minister may be a little deaf, for he had not heard my "Still, please, sir." The flash had surprised him, and he was most displeased. Although the Prime Minister's sentences were not perfectly formed, I would hazard a guess that the following might be the correct interpretation of the barks, wheezes, and grunts that made my blood run cold:

"Hey, damn you, young fellow, what the hell are you up to with your monkey tricks? Stop all this nonsense. I hate candid-camera photographs. Wait till I'm prepared, the glass of port taken away, my spectacles so, this box shut, the papers put away thus. Now then, I'm ready, but don't try any further cleverness on me!"

By degrees the Prime Minister's irritation subsided, and he settled himself to have one photograph taken and stared into the camera like some pugnacious bulldog. Click! "One more, please, sir." I walked by slow degrees and anticlockwise around the table, coming to rest finally at his left elbow. He glowered, like an oppressive cloud, into the lens as I clicked away as quickly as I could.

"Sorry I can't go upstairs for the lights, but come again another day," he said. The great man was now genial and helpful.

"Would you look this way, sir?" He turned his head obediently. Like a child waiting to get down from his chair, he kept mumbling, "I must go now. I've got to go." And again I clicked. "But come again another day." He rose from his chair.

I asked, "May I take a flash of you, sir, as you walk along the corridor outside?"

"Certainly, so long as you don't photograph me putting on my coat or hat; no fooling about!"

When my camera was in position, and my assistant ready with flashlight, the Prime Minister started his stately progress down the hall. He beamed. The flash went off twice. I moaned to the assistant, "But that was a double flash!"

The Prime Minister stopped. "What does that mean? It's ruined? Does it mean it won't come out?"

"Yes, sir."

At once Mr. Churchill turned on his heel, to walk back the length of the hall and repeat the exodus for my benefit. Lighting his cigar, he waited patiently while the assistant tried, all fingers and thumbs, to reload the flash lamp. Finally Mr. Churchill said, "I must go now." The assistant spent endless time putting in the new bulb.

"I can't wait," said the Prime Minister.

Then my assistant, at last ready, let off his flash too soon. Oblivious of this disaster, the Prime Minister, now in an excellent mood, smiled benignly at me, and I had not the heart to let him know his magnanimous gesture had been unrewarded. I was able, nevertheless, to beam with satisfaction, for although less than five minutes had elapsed since I had been admitted into the Cabinet Room, I had been able to get a good number of interesting snapshots.

A photograph I took on this occasion became one of Mr. Churchill's best-known portraits and throughout the war was to be seen in newspapers, magazines, on posters, postcards, calendars, and in the place of honour next to Their Majesties on the walls of nearly every public house in the country.

My luck continued to hold good; in many respects the war widened my horizons: I visited many battlefields. I was constantly on the move travelling to far countries which otherwise I would never have seen; my subjects never lacked in variety, ranging from life in an English munition factory to tank battles in the Libyan Desert. My Ministry of Information passes took me under the sea and into the air.

"Who goes there?"

"Friend."

"Come close and be identified. Is that a camera you have got there?"

"Yes. Er—here are—er—my—M-Ministry of Information papers."

I was often arrested and taken to the police station. At the time of the bombing of London nerves were strained and emotions very near the surface. When I was taking pictures before the dust had settled from the explosions and the fires were still burning, I would be set upon by an angry crowd who, seeing me in my civilian clothes with a Rolleiflex in my hand, considered that I was either a foreign spy or was indulging in photography as a frivolous personal whim. But most of my adventures were remarkably inspiring and sometimes, as I photographed, I would have difficulty in swallowing an emotional lump in my throat. There, in her half-demolished house, was the old actress, covered with soot from the nearby explosion, companioned by her cat and brewing herself a cup of tea after a night of terror and destruction. Long after she had been told by the police that her home was unsafe, she had insisted on salvaging her remaining possessions before she left the condemned dwelling. She seemed to mind more than anything else the loss of her dining table. She

St. Paul's Cathedral, seen
through the façade of a
bombed shop

A bombed Wren church in
the City

picked up a leg of it. "Tut, tut, tut! Just look at it. My lovely table, my lovely table all smashed to bits." Into the gaping window she proceeded to pin Queen Victoria's message: "Please understand there is no one depressed in this house, and we are not interested in the possibilities of defeat; they do not exist." Although she was forced to lodge elsewhere, for many days afterwards her faithful cat was seen taking up its habitual position on a mound of rubble in front of the fireplace still lodged in the one remaining wall of what had been her sitting room.

At the time of the most concentrated bombing of the city of London, James Pope-Hennessy and I collaborated on a survey of destroyed historical buildings. On the morning after twelve Christopher Wren churches had been burnt, James and I mountaineered over the remains of Paternoster Row to arrive simultaneously with the vicar of All Hallows to see the carcase of his church, saved from the Great Fire of 1666, but now gutted overnight; even the contents of the iron safe had been reduced to cinders. His daughter, in a tam-o'-shanter, foraged for a few relics from the altar. All that was left were a couple of cupids on the charred walls, and on one or two of the memorial plaques the mourning figures, with downcast eyes, still prayed; but one be- wildered, beheaded Elizabethan courtier, in his carved stone ruff, stared upwards through the fallen roof at the open sky above. After a heavy fall of snow these London ruins took on an even stranger aspect. Perhaps of all curious sights, the Natural History Museum provided the most sinister when a bomb explosion shattered the windows of the glass cases and the bronto- saurus and other prehistoric monsters escaped from their imprisonment.

Looking through my wartime photographs, I am reminded of many inci- dents. Here, for instance, taken at the time of the Battle of Britain, is a photograph of the R.A.F. pilots in the anteroom of the Mess—just one of many in a series, but of the men I photographed that morning, perhaps only one or two are alive now. You can see the ugly Turkey carpet, the leather and wicker chairs, the large table from which the men picked up crumpled copies of newspapers and magazines, and, over the mantelpiece, the photo- graph of the King and Queen. The C.O., that man with the tankard of beer in his fist, announced just after we had gone in to lunch that a "sweep" had suddenly been made over France and, a few moments later, the men with whom we had been drinking before lunch were already back after their adventure, chattering like starlings. While we had been eating our fish, they had shot down four German aircraft.

Here are hundreds more of the R.A.F. series; pictures of the people who fought the Battle of Britain. While I was making this snapshot of an em- barrassed pilot standing against the fuselage of his aircraft, so fair and

Bombers going out

youthful, the other pilots of his squadron shouted good-natured gibes; and he retorted, "Alone I done it!"

We were having a heat wave in England the afternoon I took these pictures.

"How about going up and taking a shot at a formation of Spitfires?" the squadron commander asked.

High above the clouds, in the crystal-clear sunlight, I felt cool and refreshed—untroubled for the first time in several days. The pictures came out well; you can even see the pilot smiling. Just after this picture was taken I finished the roll of film and put my thumb up; the pilot pulled back the stick and flashed upwards in an inverted dive, his aircraft looking like some sort of marvellous silver fish.

Here, too, are pictures of the balloon barrage, operated by men living the life of hermits throughout the changing weathers on their isolated sites.

Other pictures bring back vividly the anguish of arctic cold suffered by men whose jobs kept them around the flare path throughout the long dark nights of winter. When I look at photographs taken in the fuselage of the various types of bombers, I can still smell that curious acid-drop, pear-drop aroma which pervaded the interiors of these vast aircraft.

My photographs of Bomber Command were the results of many weeks spent among extraordinarily brave young men who knew, from the percentage of losses, that their chances of survival were small. I photographed them while, lightheartedly, almost casually, they set out to bomb Berlin. No hanging around the aircraft before the take-off. They scrambled in at the last moment as if they were catching a bus to take them in to the local cinema. Even the wireless messages they sent out while ack-ack burst around their aircraft as they droned over enemy country seemed full of confidence; and, even doomed, they retained their gaiety.

"Bombs successfully released, but natives seem to be hostile. Plane losing height over Alps. Love and kisses."

"Raid successful. Am just about to bail out. Unfortunately we seem to be above sea. Good morning."

At dawn in the crew room the survivors of the night reassembled after their return trip to Cologne. The interrogation officer at a map-strewn table, with a pencil in his hand, looked somehow more worried than the crews, who, though they appeared weary and dishevelled and rather blue about the chin, wore a look of satisfaction, an air of glory. They pulled deeply at their cigarettes and gulped the sweet souplike tea. Morning light came through the windows; black-out shutters were taken away; and at last, their story of heroism told in the most matter-of-fact terms, everyone lumbered off to breakfast and bed.

The small girl, with bomb terror still in her eyes, was sitting in her bed in the hospital, clinging to the rag doll which had survived with her. Her face, so babylike, had suddenly grown old and pale; and as I approached her bed, she looked at me in a trance of trustful misery. The resultant picture was used on the cover of *Life* magazine and, more than any other picture, was said to have influenced American feeling. It was also used as a poster in the American Red Cross campaign.

There is the whole file of photographs marked "War in the Desert." I was sent by the Ministry of Information and the Air Ministry to take photographs and make specified reports of the war in the Near East. At a time when it was impossible for most professional photographers to obtain film or flash bulbs, I embarked at Greenock, Scotland, for Freetown in West Africa with a wealth of photographic equipment and instructions to photograph anything and everything of interest I saw. Captain Homer helped me to photograph many different aspects of life on board his ship. I let off my flashes in the engine room, on the bridge, in dining rooms, dormitories, and the enormous meat safes below deck.

When I landed in Freetown and made preparations to start my photographic assignment, I met with more pigheaded opposition than I could have believed possible. Although my letters of instructions from the Ministry of Information were quite specific, they were ignored. When I said I was determined to carry out my instructions, I was arrested and released only on the definite understanding that I was forbidden to take any pictures except three miles inland. Such photographs would be of interest to no one, and instead I turned my lens on the natives in their beautiful Birmingham cotton draperies. It was like photographing a ballet. My subjects ran screaming in every direction lest I should obtain their image and subsequently stick pins into it, and I later adopted the ruse of holding the camera sideways and pretending to photograph a tree or a flower in a hedge. Then, by looking obliquely into the view finder, I would see the native, holding a bunch of frangipangi or a chicken, wonderingly approach me, and could then photograph him or her in the most graceful natural attitudes.

From the squalor and stupidity of Freetown I was eventually delivered by a plane that took me to Cairo, and a week later I was in the Libyan Desert. Confronted with the desert, where everything is on a grandiose scale —the sky, the distance, and man's behaviour—I felt incapable of translating my emotion into photographic terms. During my long professional career no problems ever perplexed me more than those I encountered when trying to

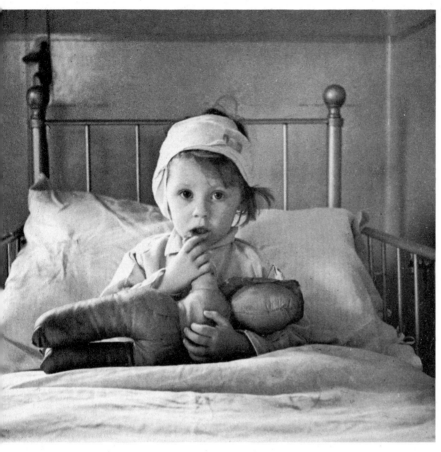

A child in a London hospital after an air raid. This picture appeared on the cover of LIFE *magazine. It was also used on an American Red Cross poster.*

Life in a shelter

take pictures of the Eighth Army. Apart from difficulties of light and atmosphere, there was the problem of sand which crept into the camera, often causing a shutter to misfire or a series of black stripes to appear on my negative, so that every evening I had to spend much time in a hermetically sealed tent, meticulously flicking every cranny of my equipment with a water-colour paintbrush. These were additional difficulties of which I was not aware until the photographic results came through and I saw how banal was the effect of many of my negatives. If, as usually happened, the sun was high and the sky innocent of cloud, my subject—whether wrecked building, tents, or machines—would be suffused with a deadening, though brilliant, light, which caused it to disappear into the background haze. Try to photograph the faces of men in the desert in most daytime conditions and they will appear black and with the crowns of their heads and the tips of their noses vividly illuminated. Photographing in a sandstorm is like photographing in a November fog. Only after dawn and just before sunset does the light provide a third dimension.

I remember in a dust storm passing a ruined bank at Sollum. Though strangely twisted and scarred by shellfire, it made comparatively little impression on me at the time; but a day later I saw the same building, wrapped in a lurid apricot evening light against a blue sea the colour of Brazilian butterflies' wings, transformed into an edifice mysterious and magical.

All picturemaking is largely a question of introducing and arranging contrasts, but this is particularly true of photography in the desert. Here contrasts of light and suitable subject matter proved equally hard to come by. Vast areas of the desert are as empty of incident as one imagines must be the surface of the moon itself. Owing to the danger of air bombardment, every hut was isolated. Seldom did one see more than a couple of lorries side by side; and human beings, their tents, and headquarters were never sufficiently close to form a composite photograph.

After one has lived for a while in the empty desert, almost anything that emerges from the mottled rubble begins to tempt one's camera. The scale is so vast, one loses a sense of proportion; and I would sometimes excitedly photograph an object looming near and large, only to discover, when the negative was developed, that it was merely a pin point object in the distance. It took me weeks to discover that whatever I photographed must be almost within arm's length. Rarely were details too close for treatment. Pictures of discharged cartridge cases, gas masks, and empty tins lying at one's feet create the most vivid impressions of modern desert warfare. The results of the concentrated bombing of Tobruk produced some peculiar patterns and textures which made successful photographs, and although I

Tank crew in the western desert

Sandstorm in the western desert

After a sandstorm

*Wreckage in
the western desert*

Tobruk Harbor

felt very weak at the time of taking them, my photographs of emergency operations in a desert hospital were extremely dramatic.

From Libya I went on to take photographs in Palestine, Syria, Iraq, and Iran. Everywhere there were opportunities. The threshing of corn, the mosques, the Garden of Gethsemane, the Arab Legion, and the various patriarchs of Jerusalem afforded wonderful material, and I sent back hundreds of rolls of film to the Ministry of Information.

In Baghdad, during a whirlwind visit in the greatest heat of the year, I took photographs of a dozen of the leading citizens, including the Regent of Iraq with little King Feisal. The King's English governess, living in this remote palace, impressed me enormously. In these surroundings she seemed eccentrically English, but it was thanks to her that the young King had such charming poise and manners. In Teheran I photographed the King and Queen of Persia (since divorced) in their modernistic house among the mountains. The King was not expecting to be recorded on gelatine and had not shaved that morning, but his beautiful Botticellian wife had attired herself for my arrival in the height of film fashion. I had wanted her to pose in early Persian costume, for I felt that she would have looked her best as a princess in a Persian or a Mogul miniature; but when I asked to see her wardrobe I was shown only peppermint-green ostrich boas, lamé tea gowns, and all the trappings of a Hollywood star.

In Teheran I was commissioned to take photographs at the British aerodrome of the American bombers arriving to be handed over to the Russians. These vast rows of planes lined up on one side of the aerodrome, before being taxied across to the far side of the strip for the final take-off, created a magnificent sight. But I had not made more than half a dozen exposures when a Russian came up and escorted me to the police. For twenty minutes an argument continued among an American press officer, a Russian woman interpreter, a Russian avaitor, and myself.

The American press officer explained: "This Ministry of Information photographer has taken the photographs on British-American ground; and, in any case, the pictures will be submitted to the censor."

"No," said the dry-mouthed Russian interpreter quite stubbornly, "the film must be liquidated."

After an hour's discussion I agreed that I would hand over my film to the American, but not to the Russian. In any case, I would go forthwith to complain to the British air attaché. It was very hot, I have seldom been more angry, and I do not like being angry, even in cold weather. While waiting for my guide to take me to the air attaché in a jeep, I stood on a terrace by the barracks, where Russian soldiers were billeted in the same house with some R.A.F. pilots. The R.A.F. entrance was in the sun; the Russians—boys of about seventeen—were sitting in the shade. I walked ten yards towards the comfort of the shade and was standing trying to pry a splinter out of a finger, thereby forgetting my ill-humour, when a Russian sentry indicated I should go back to the sun. I called the female interpreter.

"Isn't this our aerodrome? Are we not allies? I am in officer's uniform. What does this man mean by ordering me about?"

Before the woman could reply, the sentry angrily whipped out his bayonet and pointed it towards me. I did not dawdle long in front of the beady-eyed fanatic, or the interpreter, or, for that matter, in Teheran. I had seen enough of the Soviet Russians to realise I did not enjoy collaboration. Later the air attaché explained. "It's hopeless," he said. "You'll never get anywhere with the Russians. They are no more our allies than the Italians. They mistrust and hate us. Their instructions are to 'accept everything, say nothing, and distrust everyone.'" He regaled me with a succession of stories of behaviour on the part of the Russians so unbelievably bad that at this moment London and Moscow were still exchanging acrimonious letters. "But it'll lead to nothing," said the air attaché. "The other day they refused to allow us to use our own radio here, and as a result some of our aircraft crashed. But they don't care. Human life is of no account to them. You were lucky you didn't get that bayonet through your stomach."

Since so much admiration and respect was felt in England at this time for our Eastern allies, it came as a great surprise to me to discover how antagonistic was their attitude. It was impressed on me for the first time that, unless Russia was thoroughly exhausted as a result of the war with Germany after the cease-fire, we should be in for a very poor time.

When I returned to the Libyan Desert, the great German attack, so long expected, suddenly broke with great force, and for several days we were convinced it had been successfully parried. But gradually the truth dawned that all was not well and that the German advance was still assured and steady. Carefully prepared British camps had now to be destroyed as the Army fell back towards Cairo and Alexandria; and though a few optimists considered that the farther the Germans advanced, the greater would be the backswing, plans for the evacuation of Cairo were being put into execution. Black plumes of smoke were rising from burning documents as I escaped into the air and flew to Portugal en route for home.

My sudden arrival in the pretty pistachio town of Lisbon furnished one of the greatest contrasts that life has ever provided for me. To find myself amid the baroque elegancies of Portuguese life, after the primitive existence in the desert, was like living in a luxurious fantasy. I was ordered to make a record of the leading personalities of the country and of the most beautiful buildings of its wonderful little towns, and I have never enjoyed an assignment more. Fresh from the Wagnerian grandeur of the desert war, I found here the effervescent gaiety of a Mozart opera. My Portuguese pictures were silvery and gay; and, as a batch, I consider them among the most successful I have yet taken.

Cameras of any sort had become extremely scarce in England during the war, and the Ministry of Information had no spare camera to give me. Throughout the war years I travelled only with my one Rolleiflex; and if it had been broken in the desert, or at the farthest point of my wanderings, I should have been completely helpless. But, wrapped up at night in a silk handkerchief, it withstood the desert sand, finally succumbing, when the last photograph of my tour in Portugal had been taken, to a strangely Freudian accident. Subconsciously aware it was no longer of urgent use, I tripped up on a marble staircase and allowed it to sustain serious injuries.

Except on one occasion my camera always journeyed with me. Now that I had covered the war in the Near East and spent nearly a year captioning my negatives and writing notes and reports, the Ministry of Information sent me to the Far East. My photographic equipment was sent on in advance to India. A lucky decision, for the Dakota aboard which I took off from Land's End in the middle of the coldest night ever known, developed engine trouble as soon as it was air-borne and bucketed about the sky, shaking its terrified occupants like dice in a box, before crashing and bursting into flames. I was able to jump out at the last moment, but all my luggage perished.

My second attempt, however, was successful, and a few days after I had arrived in Delhi my Rolleiflex and films were safely delivered to me, and I was sent off to photograph the war on the Assam-Burma front.

Visually so different from the Libyan campaign, this type of warfare proved almost as difficult to portray photographically. My pictures gave an almost idyllic impression of sunlight filtering through the tropical trees onto Gurkhas camouflaged with leaves and exotic plants as for a festival; but they gave not even the slightest hint of the loneliness and quiet terror of jungle warfare, which first and foremost is a war of nerves, never allowing complete relaxation, so that even during the long night hours men must lie with one ear cocked, listening to the rustle of the elephant grass and attempting to distinguish between the sound of a breaking twig and an approaching footfall. At any moment a Japanese sniper might creep through the branches, to appear five feet away with a knife raised above his head.

I arrived in the month of January at the beginning of the Burmese

Arakan front, Burma: Bringing in the wounded

spring. My pictures did not reveal the fact that for nearly two thirds of the year the rain pours down incessantly and the mud becomes knee-deep, your clothes are soaked, and there is no possibility of drying them. Everything becomes coated with mould; even the bamboo props of the foxholes grow internal fungus, and the stink of decay is everywhere. Your toes begin to rot, and you feel even your brain is disintegrating. The mosquitoes thrive on English flesh; the leeches come out in their millions, waggling their black heads from side to side, or, unnoticed, furrow greedily into your skin.

For as long as six or seven years, men who before the war had lived quiet, civilised lives in England, Scotland, and Wales had been exiles in the jungle. Mail arrived irregularly, and the parcels were few and far between. No entertainment parties were sent to these forward areas and very few photographs were taken, for the Burmese campaign was not "news," and by this time the campaigners had begun to think of themselves as men of the Forgotten Army. My welcome, therefore, was so rousing that I felt, at last, that my existence in the Far East and the cost of my journey were justified. Wherever I went I was bidden to share the limited rations of food and drink. I discovered that soldiers who, month after month, had seen nothing but khaki uniforms were delighted to see someone in civilian clothing; and during much of the time I spent in the jungle I wore an old tweed suit. Faced with such enthusiasm, I could not appear tired. I worked unusually hard; and here, for instance, is my programme for January 13, 1944, the day before my fortieth birthday.

TOUR PROGRAMME—*13th Jan. 1944*

0900	Leave Div. H.Q. with Maj. MAC CASE
1030	Arrive KENNEDY PEAK
	See—2/5 Royal Gurkha Rifles
	Bty 129 Fd Regt. R.A.
	A.A. guns positions 82 A.A./A. Tk. Regt, R.A.
1130	Leave
1145	Arrive VITAL CORNER
	See—9 Border Regt.
	6 Mtn Bty
	M.M.G. pl West Yorks
1230	Leave
1245	Arrive 1/7 Gurkha Rifles

1300   Leave
1315   Arrive H.Q., 48 Bde
          Lunch
1415   Leave
1445   Arrive M.S. 68. Met by Maj. KEAN
          See—1/4 Gurkha Rifles
               Mortar Bty, 29 Mtn Regt.
1530   Leave
1545   Arrive H.Q. 63 Bde.
          Tea
1630   Leave
1645   Arrive SEIZANG
          See—A Coy West Yorks
1700   Leave
1730   Arrive TIDDIM
Note — Sappers of 70 Field Coy and Bulldozers of M.E.
          Coy will be met working on road.

I was ready to start the day's work each morning at sunrise, visiting nearby camps in the mountains, photographing men in remote gun sites, electrical engineers at the wireless units; then off in a jeep over hazardous mountain passes. Everywhere I went I wrote down the names and addresses of the men who appeared in the photographs and promised to send them a picture. By the end of the day I was dazed with sleepiness in the unaccustomed mountain air and physically exhausted by the exercise of negotiating the precipitous slopes, but I looked with satisfaction at the hundreds of captions in which my day's work was recorded:

Film No. 218.
    Sergeant H. Baxter from Peckham
    Kennedy Point—highest Ack-Ack gun site in the war—8800 ft.
Film No. 230.
    Cookhouse—West Yorks:
       Lance Corporal White, West Yorks, with SEAC writing to his wife.
    Group of 1/4 Gurkhas:
       Company sergeants packing their company's kit after preliminary moving forward.
       Brigadier hearing reports from officer returned from seven-day patrol on foot;

Lt. Col. Hedley and Brigadier R. T. Cameron looking at Jap encampments;
Dhotiyal porters working on Tiddim Road.

Every day I had some great photographic opportunities. The light had been so kind; the Indian snipers creeping through the undergrowth, or hidden in trees, had made interesting subjects. Very fortunate had been our arrival at sundown at that camp where the evening meal was being cooked and the air was hazy with smoke, for the men standing among the tree trunks cast extraordinary silhouetted shadows in the sun's rays. Later that night, in a small mud hut dug below the earth, I had sat cowering over a fire. Suddenly Colonel Dawson, who earlier in the day had described with such expert horticultural knowledge the flowers and trees of the jungle, rushed in to say that the battery at Kennedy Point was about to open up on the Japs some thousand yards away. The scramble up the mountain in the dark to the highest gun site, the muffled voices, the vaguely discernible silhouettes around the gun emplacements were extremely dramatic. When after a long silent wait the guns were eventually fired, the noise was fantastic. Gun flashes lit up an extraordinary scene that had the macabre quality of a Goya picture.

After three hours of deep sleep the next day's activities would begin. In a week I had acquired an enormous bundle of exposed negatives; and it was necessary to travel as light as possible, for the day's work entailed much hard going, crossing rivers in small boats, scrambling through the undergrowth, or climbing up steep mountainsides. I decided I would rid myself of the unnecessary burden; and by giving my films to the press-relations officer who escorted me and letting him send them back for processing to H.Q. in Delhi, I made one of the greatest mistakes of my career. I never saw the films again. They were irretrievably lost. Even Lord Louis Mountbatten's services in trying to track them down were in vain. It was of no comfort to be told that these things were always happening in India. To this day, lying awake at night, I am sometimes haunted by thoughts of the hundreds of people I disappointed and of the opportunities I squandered.

Next I flew to the Arakan front and continued my activities there. I was now conscious, as never before the war, of the advantages of notoriety. In this remote theatre it was immensely helpful. Wherever I went, a secret memo had been received giving the proposed programme.

SECRET
39 / 28 / 38 / G.S. (1)
Main H.Q. 7 Ind Inf Div
c/o 18 Adv Base P.O.
Dated 21st January, 1944

H.Q., 33 Ind Inf Bde.
H.Q., 89 " " "
H.Q., 114 " " "
Subject: *TOURS*
1.   Mr. CECIL BEATON, SEAC photographer, will be in the DIV area on 21st and 22nd Jan, accompanied by a PR offr from HQ 15 CORPS. It is hoped that MR. BEATON will have the opportunity to take photographs of personnel of as many arms and services as possible, but it is particularly desired that he should be able to visit as least one British, one Indian and one Gurkha Bn as well as units of British and Indian arty and other arms/services.
2.   The following programme has been arranged provisionally:

3.   In addition to the above programme MR. BEATON will have ample opportunity of photographing personnel of RE, RIASC, PRO etc en route.
4.   It is hoped that all units will give MR. BEATON every possible assistance during his tour.
      A/Q
      Camp (please arrange reception and accommodation DIV HQ).
      MTO (Mr. BEATON will be provided with tpt by HQ 15 CORPS).
      ADC
CF
   21/1.

Arriving at some headquarters, I would learn that the officer in charge already knew my name. This saved time and pleased us both. Telling me that his wife had often admired my pictures in the *Tatler*, he would ask me to have a drink with him, and my working schedule would be facilitated.

After some rather grim glimpses of Far Eastern warfare I returned in almost holiday mood to the comparatively peaceful atmosphere of India to photograph aspects of national, military, and cultural life. Here it was hardly possible not to take good pictures, for India gives the cameraman every kind of encouragement—brilliant contrasts of light and shade, an extraordinary kaleidoscope of patterns, flowing drapery, tinsel ornaments, and tissues, massive cloud formations seen through filigree foregrounds of palm or pepper trees, and the never-failing beauty of the inhabitants of this gigantic sub-continent, who, with their extraordinary grace and natural dignity, their elongated limbs like living bronze statues, mysterious and gazelle-like eyes, firm sensuous lips, make the perfect subjects for the camera's ruthless eye.

For six months I took hundreds of photographs every week. My opportunities included innumerable religious celebrations, the inspired haphazard colours of the Muharram and the Holi, with crowds fantastically dressed and the processions, beautiful and unaccountable, surrounding edifices of paper and tinsel and flowers. I also photographed idyllic rural scenes of the farmers using agricultural implements of a thousand-year-old design; women drawing water from the well in gourdlike pots, wearing always surprisingly graceful draperies; small boys learning to weave and, in the jute mills, female workers, as strong and noble as caryatides, bearing on their heads huge honey-coloured loads of straw; kittenlike schoolgirls in school, with magnolia complexions and wrought-gold earrings and that most personal and beautiful of all garments, the sari.

How could any photographer fail to take memorable pictures in the sculptured caves at Ellora? Or when your guide, like a genie, walks before you with a lamp to reveal the delicate cave paintings at Ajanta? Or when these paintings are reincarnated by dancers rhythmically performing their incantations by the edge of the Arabian Ocean? How could any photographer fail to be stimulated by the pearly Indian mosques and by scented flower gardens, with a magic carpet of emerald-green parrots flying past across the sky? By the life in the Rajputana villages; the coral city of Jaipur, where the dyers walk in the hot sunlight drying their lengths of magenta, puce, and yellow muslin; the holy city of Benares; the Kipling-esque Himalayan mountain stations; the grandiose life of the northwest frontier; the sinister life of Calcutta; the quayside at Bombay, or the markets in the old town of Delhi?

I now continued my travels and set forth for China. At this stage of the war's progress the only means of getting into China from India was by air. The flight "over the hump" from Calcutta to Chungking was an alarming and dangerous operation; the navigator and pilot were continually being faced with unforeseen difficulties, there were unexpected air pockets, and the electric storms over the Himalayas were often violent and sudden. Between landing stations there was little hope of making a successful forced landing; even the touch-down at Chungking between two mountain gorges was in itself a feat.

Our flight was comparatively smooth, and I was lulled into a feeling of false security by many doses from a bottle containing belladonna that I had with me, for since my flying accident it was an excruciating experience for me to have to sit in any airplane. It took me several days to recover

Ajanta caves, Hyberabad. These caves contain a record of nine centuries of Indian painting.

In a Bengali village

Rice cultivation, Bengal

The Jain Temple, Calcutta

Self-portrait, taken in the Jain Temple

A Chinese coolie

A man's face in a Chengtu
street

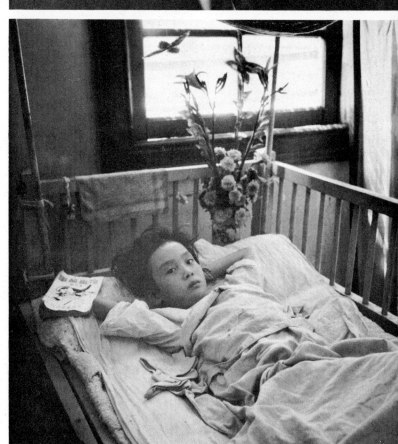

At the Canadian mission
hospital, Chengtu

from the nervous strain of this trip, although, mercifully, it was not until later that I was told that Japanese aircraft had attempted to intercept us. But before I had time to settle in my new and very strange surroundings I was taken on a three months' journey by lorry as near as possible to the front line.

For weeks on end an alarm clock would call us at four o'clock in the morning for another day's journey towards our far goal. Some hours later, after the usual, but always unexpected, delays, we piled our lorries with our bedding and mountains of baggage, to bounce and bang over potholes and boulders as we semicircled through vast mountain passes. The incredible beauty of the landscape, with the mountains as impossibly unreal as those in early Chinese decorations, the trees of wild rose, pummelo, and tung all in full flower, and the good humour of the incessantly toiling coolies were compensation for much of the discomfort, squalor, and disappointment of the long journey.

Everywhere we passed I was impressed by the hard fight for survival that the ordinary Chinese must wage against nature. In the fields the labourers were treading large wheels and defying the laws of gravity by driving the water uphill, were weeding, with their bodies bent double, the rice swamps, or stamping down the rice shoots into the bog of the paddy fields. Along the desolate roadways we would pass the cavalcades of carrier-coolies with their heavy loads of rice, salt, coal, or lead, drawn on squeaking cartwheels, the men with the muscles of calf and thigh as strongly developed as a wrestler's. Travelling by van and lorry over such rough roads was an extremely exhausting business; but this means of travel gave me an opportunity to photograph the country at close range. I even developed a technique of photographing with snapshot or moving-picture camera scenes of village life from the back of the lorry as we moved along, so that the inhabitants were not able to crowd in upon me with overwhelming curiosity.

The more I learned about the way the nation was being governed under Generalissimo Chiang Kai-shek, the more I regretted the aid that was coming to him from his allies. Everywhere I went I saw further examples of abuse of power, wanton cruelty, callousness, and corruption. I longed to leave the country and felt embarrassed at being beholden to some Chinese press official of the general's staff. I suffered tortures from the interminable delays and oriental procrastination. Part of my job consisted of photographing the important war leaders. To wait while their secretaries made an appointment and then for that appointment to be kept was a most exasperating lesson in self-control. War-stricken China showed no sense of time. A bridge would be down, so maybe one waited two weeks before crossing a river. Eventually our lorries arrived at our goal, and I spent some weeks at the British Military Mission outpost. Some of these days were not without charm and enjoyment, and my camera subjects were always fascinating.

One morning we were bid to watch a tactical exercise given by the Chinese surprise troops. The morning was funny though dangerous, and I very nearly became a casualty when a horde of Chinese boys, covered with green leaves, were set to rush about a mountainside firing at one another's backsides. When the delayed-bomb explosions for which we waited so patiently finally went off, complete disorganisation overtook the Chinese Army. "Don't laugh, chaps," said a companion, "or the Chinks will be frightfully hurt." General Li Mo-an was complimented on the programme he had staged and was about to drive off in glory, when his motor failed to move. Dozens of willing helpers shoved the vehicle, but still it would not move of its own accord. A mechanic came along with a small medicine bottle of alcohol and gave the engine a whiff and, just as the general, in a fury, was about to step out, the motor shot forward in a cloud of smoke and pebbles.

By the end of each day I had taken several movies and hundreds of still photographs, and often I would come back almost blinded with headache, so that I took to my board bed with aspirin and my overcoat, trusting that by dawn I might have slightly recovered.

The Chinese scenery, with its strange formations of the distant mountains, the neat pattern of rice fields, the tumbling, rambling blossoming of the wild rose trees, the small village streets flanked by huge hieroglyphics painted on scabrous walls, made me into a landscape photographer for the first time. In villages, especially near Kunming and in Fukien and Kiangsi provinces, it was impossible not to take any picture that was not beautiful. But there was too much in China at that time to make one deeply wretched.

All the most beautiful towns of China were in Japanese hands, but even in as remote a town as Kweilin one saw the infiltration of the "modern style" in architecture. The old walled city was considered antiquated, and the walls were now being pulled down; in their place imitation Spanish palaces and modernistic banks and cinemas were being built. I was told that no rich merchant would dream of building himself a Chinese house, so that this hideous *style moderne* has even overrun China.

Although I was not able to witness in unoccupied China any of the life which travellers had so much enjoyed before the war, I could see the wonderful qualities of the Chinese people themselves. I loved photographing this gay and courageous people who work out their fate with such patience, courage, and even gaiety. Every type of Chinese seems to have the plastic beauty that is entirely photogenic, whether he is an old member of the government, a scholar or professor at the universities, a poverty-stricken poet, or a child with a fluttering paper fan. All street vendors, gymnasts and archers, the actors and actresses in the Ancient Chinese Theatre, the factory hands making cigarettes, and in the cotton mills the spinners of silk with their deft bird-claw hands, or the small children in the kindergarten school evacuated to a disused Buddhist temple in some remote province, all are wonderful photographic models. Some sights were so moving that tears prevented me from focussing the picture in the ground-glass view finder; and I shall never forget photographing the Red Cross hospital in Changsha.

When I had completed my mission for the Ministry of Information in the Far East, I managed to arrange a journey home via the United States. After a week's hitch-hiking by air, the arrival at Miami was extraordinarily impressive. To see the glittering lights from the sky after long-drawn years of black-out gave me the same sort of excitement that as a child I felt leaving boarding school for the holidays after my first term. Even in the cheapest quarters of the town the Miami shops were filled with so many good things that one realised to what a poor standard of living conditions we had all become accustomed.

Miami can be rather an unattractive place, even during the sunny months of winter. It was now August; the heat was tremendous, and only those who could not escape remained. To me it was bliss. When eventually I got a lift from Miami to New York, I was in a condition of ecstasy. I remained on Manhattan in dazed delight for three weeks.

During this time I went back to my prewar photography with a newly acquired abandon. The affluence and fantastic luxury that I had to portray delighted me. Yet my recent experiences in photographing some of the grimmer aspects of life had had an influence, perhaps only a temporary one, on my work. Even in the fashion pictures I took I tried to evolve a greater simplicity and deeper feeling of reality. I photographed an exquisite New York mannequin wearing a frown and spectacles as she did her sewing.

"This is the 'new reality,'" said the *Vogue* editors.

Later one evening the beauty editor of a rival magazine asked me what I thought would be the next trend in fashion photography.

"I feel it is towards a greater sense of reality," I stuttered, and went on to explain that I considered there was something a bit ridiculous about models being determinedly artificial. Most of them were photographed in the impersonal backgrounds of a studio and continued to appear so unimaginably chic that it was impossible to believe they had any life of their own—or were, in fact, live people.

"That's an interesting thought," said the beauty editor.

A week later at her conference on the beauty issue this editor suggested it would make a wonderful cover to show a young woman at the hairdresser just about to go into the dryer with her curls in pins. The idea was dashed to pieces by the other editors.

"Oh no! How ugly, how inelegant! That would never do! You must be crazy!"

But the beauty editor was stubborn and sadly shook her head as she said, "After all, it is reality we're after, isn't it?"

While I was in New York I heard of the liberation of Paris. The final defeat of Germany could not be far away. I went back to England with a tremendous number of war photographs to caption; but I knew that my work for the Ministry of Information would soon be at an end, and I believed that at last I should have a long respite from photography. But this was not to be. I doubt if I shall ever entirely cease being a photographer.

Before the war was over I went to France to photograph Churchill visiting the snow-covered front lines. In Paris I found myself, more enthusiastically than ever, after the long interim, photographing my old friends Bérard, Cocteau, Picasso, and Gertrude Stein. When at last peace was declared, there were so many more wonderful opportunities for taking pictures that I found myself launched into the postwar period with its sudden rejuvenescence of activity, its new discoveries and approach, and its New Look.

Chapter 9 SOME PAINTERS AND WRITERS AND OTHERS

I HAVE been told that Queen Alexandra, each time she visited Thomas Downey, the photographer, used to ask, "Do you think I am putting on a little weight?" She knew that he, the photographer, better than her friends, seeing his sitter only at intervals, could take stock of any change. But perhaps this dear lady did not know that the photographer, working in the relentless light of the studio, sees the changes almost before they are about to happen, certainly before they are seen by the rest of the world. For the photographer of long experience, it is one of the saddest aspects of his job to have to photograph the same woman, year after year, to watch the magic quality of youth disappearing, and give way to complete *dégringolade*.

Occasionally, however, the photographer is recompensed by the spectacle of some woman, who in youth visibly possessed little distinction, attaining through her experiences of life and nobility of character a beauty which no younger person could possess.

Through watching my sitters under the harsh lights of the studio I have learned more about them in one brief hour than if we were to meet on a dozen different social occasions. By their attitude towards the proceedings so much of their character is revealed; vanity, self-assurance, sense of proportion are all exposed. Sometimes one can see through the mask that is worn for the world, and the face, now bereft of animation, is determined and cruel. At other times, the mask is dropped, and the face that is generally wreathed in smiles appears devastatingly sad. The eyes reveal much, and often I have noticed that the tragedy which at other times is kept hidden is now nakedly on view. I have felt that I should not have been witness of such private melancholy, and have later comforted myself that perhaps there is consolation for my sitters that their sorrow has become habitual.

Photography has given me a passport into many fields of interest which would otherwise have remained unknown. It has enabled me to meet, even if only once, a large variety of people. Many an afternoon have I enjoyed in isolated intimacy with some personage whose path, had it not been for my profession, I might never have crossed. Sometimes I was never to see them again; but photography has also been the means of discovering lifelong friends. Perhaps my meeting with Matthew Smith comes in the former category.

It was during the war, when Smith had been moved from Paris and was living in London, that I had arranged to meet him for the purpose of including him in a series of pictures I was to take of English painters. Although he was diffident about being photographed, it took only a certain amount of persuasion for him to agree to lunch with me; and then, if all went well, he admitted he might come along later to the studio. After seeing so many of his robust paintings of meaty great nudes and violently sensuous "still lifes," I had expected Matthew Smith to be a perfect Herculean. How very different from my imaginings was the pale, thin, and wiry little individual, peering like a small animal through thick glasses, whom I found waiting for me on the steps of the restaurant where we had planned to meet. A first encounter is often like a double interview; but this was no interview, for, seated before me, this wisp of a man kept up a running commentary—perhaps a sign of nervousness—as he poured his heart out to me.

Smith was living in a flat at 144 Piccadilly at the time. This seemed to be a strange block of flats for him to choose for his abode, and I asked him if he had decided to live there on account of the wonderful view from the windows which overlooked the park.

"Oh no!" he replied. "An artist is always given a back room without any view. I was once in Venice only for one day, and I overlooked a high dark wall. In Maida Vale, where I have my studio, there are some lovely houses, but mine is hideous—no possibilities, no proportion, no view!"

Before the war he lived in Aix-en-Provence, unfortunately never in one of those beautiful eighteenth-century houses of silver stone, but in a succession of ugly hotel bedrooms. Matthew Smith was so forthcoming that I thought perhaps he would talk to me about his methods of painting, and I tried to bring the talk around to this topic.

"Work in progress is so difficult to discuss," he said. "What I'm doing now may be experimental; it is different from the stuff I did in France before the war—the colours less vivid. Changes of life, light, and environment influence my work, and emotional crises bring about tremendous reactions. Now," he complained, "I am completely knocked off my perch without that piece of material which I always use for my backgrounds. I came across it accidentally many years ago when I saw it lying on a bed; and it's been the background for all my paintings ever since—that and a screen I designed. Now I am stranded without the piece of material and the screen; they are in France, and God knows if I shall ever see them again. I look everywhere but can't find anything that compares. Just occasionally in life one sees some colour combination that pleases—three colours hung up in a shop that one would never have thought of. But oh, what one has to contend with during a war! The difficulty of getting the right quality paint! My people have written to say they are closing down, so I've ordered a great quantity of Venetian or Titian yellow. It's lovely for skies; for white—it's yellow so pale that it looks transparent. I paint while the paint it wet; a picture is finished for me once the paints are dry; but that means an appalling amount of concentration while the picture is in progress. I paint my picture at one sitting, and get so exhausted that sometimes for three days afterwards I'm ill in bed, racked by appalling pains, and then when I get up and find the picture is no good, I become so depressed that I wonder is it all worth while."

The frail and delicate hands trembled a little as he talked. He was exceedingly depressed at the time and was only just beginning to recover from the tragic death of his two sons in the Air Force. Although the war was now going well for us, Smith said, "Now, each time there is such good news, I feel so sad that my sons aren't able to rejoice at the turn of events." One of his sons in particular had such a zest for life; there was no one, he said, in the whole world who could put so much relish and enjoyment into the word "delicious."

When at our luncheon we had reached the coffee stage I broached the question of photography, but Smith was still reluctant to discuss it.

"Couldn't we put it off," he asked, "until another day?" He told me that what should be done today he always likes to put off till tomorrow. But I was firm, and eventually I dragged him to the studio; and the sitting was as gay as it can only be when a real personality is involved.

Smith, like Graham Sutherland and many other first-rate painters I have known, disapproves of painters being photographed complete with overall, palette, and brushes, so I photographed him in the late Victorian manner with cloak and stick. Although he knew that in the results he would be "over-hatted," he wore the large felt Trilby which comes down onto his nose like a candle snuffer. I am glad that I was able to spend one afternoon with this remarkable artist.

It was entirely through my photography that I became friendly with

Picasso. I had rather dreaded going to see the man whose work I admire above all other modern painters, and on my way I conjured up mental pictures of some extremely *farouche* bohemian living in a disordered studio and expected to find the maestro in a chaos of tubes of paint and plaster. Instead of this, Picasso welcomed me to his flat in the Rue de la Boétie looking as neat as a new pin in an extremely smart navy-blue suit, white shirt which showed a lot of cuff, and a satin tie. He showed me around an apartment which contained many exquisite pieces of Regency furniture with the manner of a *grand seigneur*.

When he saw I was appreciative of the strange assortment of objects he had amassed around him, he became as enthusiastic as an excited schoolboy and showed me his favourite possessions—folding library steps, the mahogany dining-room chairs, his sculpture of a harlequin head, his "mobiles," and his collection of matchboxes. Further encouraged by my enthusiasm, he took me into his drawing room and uncovered the many armchairs which he had just upholstered in satin of brilliant Spanish colours—royal blue, emerald green, daffodil ochre, and crimson. His eyes sparkled with delight as he showed his early paintings, including Ingres-like canvases of his first wife, and his other favourite Picassos, all framed in bright gold bolection mouldings.

As sometimes happens when in the presence of certain forceful characters, I soon found I had fallen so much under Picasso's influence that I was seeing the world with eyes other than my own, with Picasso's eyes, in fact. I began to realise that many ordinary objects, pieces of cork, or metal and paper, even ordinary boxes of matches—yellow, blue, and black—which one sees every day, when seen in his company, look as if they are the creation of the master himself. That day I took hundreds of photographs of Picasso, and he showed such delight and amusement at the results that, like a child, he kept asking me to give him more and more prints.

When a few weeks after the liberation of France I called on Picasso for the first time after the long interval of the war, he remarked that I had not changed, except that my hair had become grey-white. He, too, had gone white—"How horrible!" He didn't reconcile himself to his appearance. Did I? No! He agreed. It wasn't as if one changed—as if a chair became a piano; it was the *dégringolade* that was so awful! Perhaps, as he wasn't a cinema star, it didn't matter a lot. But oh how he hated looking glasses!

Picasso was now living on two floors above a small winding Cinderella staircase in the Rue des Grands Augustins. On the vast floor space were pieces of sculpture and some of the pictures he had been doing during the war. At one end of the room, unexpectedly, was a large group of people whom I discovered were American G.I.s. At the sudden influx of another busload of people I asked him, "How can you possibly work under such conditions?"

"Oh, it is the victory. It is terrible. I cannot do any work since the victory. It has been too big, too sudden—the floods have arrived." But he talked calmly to his visitors, with great politeness and frankness of manner, and he was obviously amused and delighted with his own great success.

I brought out my camera and photographed him as we wandered from room to room. We photographed in the bedroom and bathroom, and he was amused by the unexpected things I liked to photograph. Although he had already given me a considerable amount of his time, I then asked if I might draw him. He did not seem optimistic about the prospect, but nevertheless sat very still. Later he got up to light a cigarette and had a look at my sketch. He was enthusiastic, and at once went back to sit patiently. By degrees he started to talk; about the strangeness of the G.I.s, another batch of whom were at that moment making a tour of his other rooms. He told me how they were apt to leave behind them hidden presents for him, and days later, while going around his rooms, he would find unexpected caches of soap, tea, and sugar.

My friendship with Gertrude Stein and Alice B. Toklas is also one that I owe to my camera. I had met these remarkable ladies in the company of Edith Sitwell in Paris on a momentous occasion when the three great literary figures became reconciled after a long bout of armed neutrality. I had been extremely impressed by the warmth and simplicity of this American couple, who showed such a passionate interest in everything that was going on around them. But it was when they came to London for the first night of Gertrude's ballet, *The Wedding Bouquet,* that I first photographed them and, as a result of one long morning spent together in the studio, became a devoted admirer and deeply grateful friend of both Alice and Gertrude, who were like newly found fairy godmothers and gave me so much sympathetic encouragement.

When Gertrude and Alice arrived at my studio on that memorable summer morning, they at once displayed enormous delight in all the effects I had planned as properties and backgrounds for their special sitting. I had bought patterned wallpapers which, it transpired, were like those in their apartment in Paris. The twists of electric wire hanging from on high reminded them of a mobile Picasso had made for them.

They were quite a startling-looking couple; Gertrude with her closely cropped iron-grey hair, in her flowered waistcoat and tweed skirt, Alice in a large black felt hat and grey flannel suit. In whatever juxtaposition

Gertrude Stein and Alice B. Toklas

Christian Bérard

André Gide

I took them the effect was incongruous and strange; yet so great was the integrity of their characters that they could not possibly be made to look ridiculous. About Gertrude there was always something monumental. Her magnanimity shone through her trusting brown eyes, so that she was the best sitter any photographer could ever hope to have. I was able to take many pictures of her at various stages of our friendship; I photographed her at Bilignin in her enchanting grey stone house among the poplar trees (where I stayed with her until the outbreak of war parted us), walking round the garden with Basket, her poodle, or rocking to and fro in her chair on the terrace while Alice did her needlepoint from designs by Picasso, prepared the salad for luncheon, or picked the hibiscus and tea roses for her very wonderful and personal flower arrangements.

After the long interval of war I went to seek out Gertrude and Alice in their apartment in Paris in the Rue Christine, and I was pleasantly surprised to find them both full of enthusiasm and none the worse for the experience of the dreadful years between. They were enthralled by the visits of a great number of G.I.s who had found their way there to pay their homage.

Gertrude said with evident pleasure in her warm nasal monotone, "It's quite ex-tra-ordinary the way those boys come to see us. They come to see Pablo, and they come to see me. They don't go to anybody else, and I don't believe they come to see us because we're celebrities, but because we're rebels. They know Pablo and I have had to put up a fight in our time, and we've won, and that gives them a fellow feeling, and a link. They know we can understand their problems, and so, of all people in Paris, they come to Pablo and to me—and we're both very pleased they do—and we think that we can help them with their problems, in their loneliness and independence, and, if they haven't got preconceived ideas that are too strong, then I think we can, and do, help them. But I tell some of them to go away. They've become set in their ideas, and I can't put up with anybody who has set ideas, with anyone who is *parti pris*."

The most poignant photographs are of Gertrude taken only a few weeks before she died. She seldom talked of her illness, and her friends were not encouraged to enquire after her health; but she knew that she was very ill, and the photographs show how great a drain her illness had made upon her physique. In one, where she is leaning meditatively out from the window, it seems as if she were already looking into another world.

André Gide was another whose acquaintance I made through my determination to include him among my sitters. One morning when in Paris I went to call upon this strict Protestant who had always found it difficult to reconcile his life with his Church, whose advanced outlook may at one time have been too much for society, but who now was acclaimed throughout France as one of the country's most venerable assets.

The morning I went to see Monsieur Gide I found him wearing a velvet smoking jacket and velvet slippers. He is a dandy in the matter of dress, an enthusiastic wearer of almost exaggeratedly English clothes, to which he gave an air of great fantasy. Thus to a Harris tweed coat he added piquancy by wearing it with a variety of skullcaps, smoking caps, and draped headgear. The morning we met he mooned about the apartment, showing me his possessions and completely ignoring the many bells that rang. Telephone bells and doorbells went unanswered, and the apartment therefore enjoyed an unusual calm. I could hear Gide's stertorous breathing, which reminded me of the tick-tock of the alarm clock in Captain Hook's crocodile. While I photographed and drew him, he rolled his own cigarettes and read *Suetonius*.

I was impressed by the fact that, like all great people, he said exactly what he meant and that his frankness was never resented. Gide knew just what he wanted of life, and one wish was that he should be allowed his privacy. An overenthusiastic admirer of his once tried to buttonhole him. Carefully Gide placed a chair between the lady and himself. At last, seeing she was having little success, the lady extended a hand. "Well, well," she suggested, "we'll meet again very soon." Gide, leaning on the chair and shaking his head at the lady, replied, "Perhaps." Even at the possibility of such a faint hope the lady seemed contented.

Jean Cocteau is always a most rewarding sitter. With astonishing charm and a childlike wish to please, he is perhaps the most unself-conscious person I have ever met, and possibly the most enthusiastic. He enjoys being photographed and radiates exuberance until the camera clicks, when his face suddenly assumes an expression of almost demented gravity, his strained eyes seem to be peering at some unseen horror, and his mouth becomes a knife slit. His tremulous brittle hands, metal-crisp with tapering, slightly backward-bending fingers, with discoloured, sometimes grubby nails, are intensely photogenic, as is his paper-thin body with its sparrow-claw feet.

I often feel it is a pity to ask people whose homes have such individuality of atmosphere to leave their shells and come to the anonymous background of a studio to be photographed. Cocteau's own home, whether it is one room in a hotel or a house in the country, is always filled with the appurtenances of his own special magic. In the darkness of the rooms your eyes gradually recognize the drawing boards with chalked messages and dates, the plaster masks with wax tears imposed, the "life masks" of his head and hands, the crimson wall, and the organisation of disorder; piles of letters, or photographs in portfolios, and pornographic postcards with tinsel and feathers attached. He knows where every object is to be found; the high desk for drawing, the table with equipment for smoking by his monklike pallet.

Whenever I have photographed him at his home, the magician has been discoursing and conjuring with ideas and giving such a wonderful show of wit, intelligence, and frenzied vitality that I have found it hard to interrupt in order to get on with my work. Take Cocteau away from his own atmosphere, and something is necessarily lost; but so fertile is his imagination that even in a studio he invents a succession of striking ideas for the photographer's benefit. Every minute he is assuming a pose to illustrate some jest, and with his own particular legerdemain he transfigures the well-worn properties he finds lying about.

One of the most photogenic personalities I have encountered during my whole photographic career was the late Christian Bérard. There never was taken a bad photograph of Bébé. Yet how many thousands of times he was photographed. How much he enjoyed being photographed. He was in his element posing for pictures; whenever a camera was near, he bathed in serene pleasure. Being photographed was a second métier for him. He improvised a thousand different attitudes, played as many new camera roles, and gave point to certain extraordinary objects that he would produce to be photographed with. He posed as an early Victorian painter might pose for his official portrait, as Sarah Bernhardt or Victor Hugo or Boni de Castellane would pose for the firm of Nadar. He would assume the posture of a Degas ballet dancer or be photographed with all the romantic aura of a faded snapshot of Verlaine; or, without losing his individuality, he would submit to the polishing in an over-life-size "head" by Manuel Frères for a display in the vestibules of Paris clubs or theatres.

Yet in all these hundreds of photographs Bébé looked exactly like himself; the force of his personality broke through; and his eyes, perhaps the most beautiful eyes of any man of our century—so brilliant and birdlike, yet understanding and compassionate—were alive and wonderful in every print on sensitised paper.

During the many years of our friendship I must have photographed him on thirty different occasions, in all manner of garb, with and without beard. Always he invented some further entertaining conceit or setting for himself. The most curious of all was during a summer holiday spent at Tamaris in the South of France, when we discovered an abandoned theatre with stage-set, painted drop curtain, and musical instruments. Here, with a megaphone worn as a dunce's cap, Bébé was inspired to perform a most re-

Colette, Palais Royal, Paris

markable harlequinade with the instruments of the departed dance band.

After the war I went again to photograph Colette. I had not seen her since the unsuccessful sitting when I had first gone to Paris to work for *Vogue*. Now she was living in an apartment with waist-high windows looking on to the gardens of the Palais Royal, the walls cluttered with sentimental bric-a-brac, butterflies in frames, Doré paintings, floral calendars, and water colours of herbaceous borders. Colette now spent most of her time in bed, and I brought out my Rolleiflex to snap her as she lay propped up on pillows and cushions and covered with mountains of rugs and hot-water bottles. The atmosphere was like that of any old actress's or clairvoyant's bed-sitting room. On her bed desk were nine fountain pens, dozens of sharpened pencils, and sheets of blue note paper on which her large handwriting seemed mostly to be crossed out. With her powdered face, grey frizzy hair, and dark painted eyes, her simian gestures and grand manner, she was so fascinating that she completely reconciled me to the onslaught of old age. While she talked fervently and intensely, I kept snapping the camera.

"I am writing my memoirs," she said. "It is terrible! I am writing like a monster without stop, and it's so hard—such hard work because I must expurgate one half and invent the other."

All the time she talked she gesticulated wildly. I clicked the lens with great enjoyment, knowing that I was getting excellent material. When the results came out and I compared these last photographs with the earlier ones I had taken, I was comforted by the thought that perhaps in the years between, even if my photographs themselves had not developed, I had acquired a wider appreciation and understanding of my subjects.

Another writer whom I enjoy photographing is Truman Capote. The first time I ever met Truman Capote I was surprised to discover what a very different person he seemed to be from the boy who, like a small barn owl, peered out from under a blond fringe on the back of his best-selling novel, *Other Voices, Other Rooms*. When I was introduced to him in New York one winter, I discovered him to be a kind of giant, even though he stood only five feet tall. His jaw jutted, his eyes, through thick glasses, pierced one with an intense scrutiny, and his stocky legs were planted well apart. Later, during one rainy spell the following summer in England, when he came to stay with me in my house in the country, we talked for many hours on end.

It was still his aggressive, rocklike force of intelligence and physique that impressed me rather than his feckless and intransigent youth; and I saw him as a young troglodyte, a baby Hercules. With the intention of giving this impression, I got out my Rolleiflex. The rain had been lashing down all the morning, and angry gusts of wind banged the roses against the windowpanes. It was too dark indoors to take photographs without special lights; and, as it continued to be stormy and cold outside, I asked Truman if he would mind going onto the terrace and, in the comparative shelter near the house, looking through the windowpanes at my camera trained on him from indoors. He complied and stumped out of the room. I had to shout my instructions to him very loudly as the storm raged.

"Nearer!"

"What?" he bellowed back with a volume of sound that was remarkable. "What?"

"Nearer! Come close into the window and lean against the wall."

"Wait one second," he yelled as he screwed up his face in a devilish grimace. "I'm not ready. Have to take my glasses off."

I watched in the ground glass of the camera as, very carefully, his jaw thrust forward, lower lip protruding, he removed his glasses and put an elbow against the wall. Then he looked myopically in my direction. I watched a complete transformation. I have never before seen anyone change so visibly before my eyes. The face suddenly became that of a twelve-year-old boy. The strength had gone, and in its place was the serenity of youth itself. The eyes became large and wistful; the lips had a pretty pout like the mouth in an eighteenth-century French pastel; the whole physiognomy assumed a marble-like calm. The intelligence of the writer was abandoned, while a silly, pretty photogenic façade presented itself to the camera lens.

For some minutes I continued to gaze with amazement in the ground glass. This was an entirely different character from the person to whom I had been talking! I could hardly believe my eyes, but I went on clicking the shutter. After I had taken a number of pictures I felt I, too, must come out of doors to see if this illusion existed only through the windowpanes. I was determined to photograph him as I saw him first, as a young giant. Perhaps if I tried to take some profile shots I would get an indication of the force that had impressed me so much. But I was unsuccessful. While the process of photography was on hand, the Truman Capote who proffered himself was a little gazelle-eyed waif.

Later, when I told him how surprised I had been by the metamorphosis which I had witnessed, he explained that, whenever confronted by a camera, he put on a special camera face which he knew was not his own but was his public's idea of him. A few years ago, before he was twenty, a large photograph of Truman Capote appeared in the pages of *Life* magazine which made him look like a kitten; and readers wondered how this could possibly be the author of his fantastic and macabre stories. The mystery created, Truman Capote decided to preserve it; his private self he likes to keep aloof, while he has acquired the faculty of being able to come out in a photograph looking just the way he wishes.

In general I try to arrange as many sittings as possible during one visit to the studio. Sometimes, thanks to a variety of sitters, the time passes very agreeably; and I find an extract in my diary which gives an impression of a single morning in London as varied and stimulating as at a vaudeville theatre.

My first sitter was Michael Tippett, the composer. As usual, I was a little late getting to the studio and, as usual, suffered anguish at not being on time. Tippett was sleeping in a chair awaiting my arrival. I apologised profusely and gave all the reasons for my tardiness, but he was not put out at my delay. He blinked open his dark pansy-like eyes, smoothed his fringe of dark shaggy hair, and was ready to take an interest in anything that might follow. During the sitting I found him sensitive, highly strung, and somewhat inclined to giggle. Then in marched Bill Astor to be photographed for his Conservative campaign. He was assured, and he has a sly sense of humour. During some of the pictures I took, his eyes seemed to pop out of his face.

"Please don't stare," I asked him.

"How shall I not stare? Think of sex?"

"Yes."

The result was successful.

Then General Bob Laycock. He was out of his element. This lion-brave soldier twitched with discomfort and was thoroughly ill at ease throughout the ordeal.

Then Esmond Rothermere arrived.

"Are you in a hurry for these photographs?" I asked.

"No!" He laughed. "We've already been a year trying to arrange this sitting."

He is such a good-looking and essentially youthful-looking man that it is unfortunate that he is unphotogenic. Or is it that I have no talent for, or conviction about, photographing him? I cannot get his great charm into any of my pictures.

My last arrivals before luncheon were Madge Elliott and Cyril Ritchard—he in top hat and tails, she in spangled skirt and fake gardenias—like a team of entertainers at a piano for a children's party. They are a disarming and delightful couple of troupers. They love one another very dearly, and in spite of their success, or perhaps it is the reason for it, they have a way of inviting one's sympathy.

T. S. Eliot is the only person I can bring to mind who has ever refused to be counted among my sitters. He explained that it would be impossible to decide what sort of collar he should wear for the pictures; a soft one would look untidy and bohemian, and yet he could not bring himself to be perpetuated in a starched one.

Nor did I ever photograph George Bernard Shaw. I met him at luncheon at Lady Lavery's house, and he had agreed to sit for me. One day Miss Joseph, my secretary, was surprised by his sudden arrival in our house.

"I've come to be photographed," he explained.

"But Mr. Beaton's out! Did he expect you?"

"No! But I thought photographers were always in," said the great man as he left, never to return.

Chapter 10 PHOTOGRAPHING ROYALTY

I N T H E whole range of people who must regularly submit to being photographed, my experiences with royalty have been the most pleasant. Politicians of other periods were decorative, often somewhat picturesquely dressed creatures, with their strange hats, collars, and buttonholes; but during my own career they have proved, as a general rule, ugly, cantankerous, and obviously pressed for time. Most film stars, though necessarily photogenic, are too silly, or too young, to be interesting subjects for a photographer, and the older ones know too much about how they wish to present themselves to the public to give him free rein. But whenever a sitting has been arranged with a royal personage, and I may have feared that the occasion might prove difficult, my sitter has been good-tempered and helpful and has always adopted a professional attitude towards the procedure. Although it is important that royalty should be dignified, they are more courageous and show greater confidence in the photographer than any other sitters.

Maybe some older members of certain royal families still think of a cameraman in terms of late Victorian photography; and sometimes I have detected surprise at my approach to the problem. Watching me arrange elaborate décors for their pictures, "How strange that he puts himself to such trouble," I seem to hear them say. "So long as the pictures are flattering, who cares? And in any case, all these backgrounds and flowers—what does it mean?" But now that press photography of royalty has become a part of daily life, many younger members of the royal family know exactly how best to face the onslaught of the camera and instinctively pose to the greatest advantage when confronted by a battery of press photographers; the Duchess of Kent knows when to lower her chin, Princess Margaret when to raise hers.

My first sitter of royal stock was the elderly Princess Louise, Duchess of

Argyll, a daughter of Queen Victoria, whom I photographed in our drawing room in a variety of conventional period poses in a grey tea gown. She was a charming old lady with pale hair and features, but it was difficult to register her personality with my Folding Kodak. However, after a lengthy exchange of correspondence, one picture among many was chosen as the favourite. The photograph had already received a great deal of attention when I received the following letter (it may be pointed out that the Princess was herself an artist of considerable prowess):

DEAR MR. BEATON,

Her Royal Highness says the alterations have been beautifully done; only the following remarks were made:

Owing to the delicacy of the whole picture, the cheek should not be so light against the deep shadow left side, as also the eye; the bone above eye requires slightly turning down; the right eye should be a tiny bit bigger towards the nose, upper lid. The nostril on left-hand side would not show in that position, and makes the nose look a little out of drawing. The bright light on the left eye is a tiny bit too strong.

Can the straight line down the left side (where the shoulder has been very well rectified) be a little less sharp, to attract the eye less? When looking at the picture it attracts too much, but Her Royal Highness knows this must have been troublesome. The hair to be a wee bit lighter. You may notice the Princess has lightened it a little in parts.

Later I received an addendum from the lady in waiting:

Did I in the note ask you not to have too much light on the nose as it is inclined to make it too prominent H.R.H. thinks?

The Duke of Kent was one of my early patrons; and although sometimes he seemed critical of the results, he was so amused at the amateur way in which I performed the ritual of photography with the assistance of Ninnie, the nurse, Miss Joseph, my secretary for many years, and Manley, the butler, to be interrupted, perhaps, by the unexpected return of my father from the City, that he enjoyed coming back to watch more family histrionics.

When the Duke was engaged to be married, he entrusted the beautiful and mysterious-looking Princess Marina to my photographic care, and a new star of classical beauty appeared in my hierarchy. I could never bear to call a halt to any sitting. I photographed the Duchess in national Greek costume, in shepherdess hats and Ascot hats, in tiaras, and in a variety of different hairdressings; and of the hundreds of pictures I have taken of the Duchess, my favourites are those in which she wears a Winterhalter crinoline against a background of feathery trees, though the Duchess's preference is for simpler effects and, in particular, for a photograph in which she resembles a fine fragment of Greek statuary.

During the war I photographed the Duke many times when he was visiting various R.A.F. stations, and I was bidden to Coppins one summer afternoon to take pictures of the Duke and Duchess with the newly born Prince Michael; but these proved to be tragic pictures, for they were the last official photographs of the Duke before he was killed a few days later in an air tragedy in Scotland.

One evening in July 1939 a cheerful voice on the telephone asked, "Is that Mr. Beaton?" When reassured, it continued, "It's the lady in waiting speaking, and the Queen wants to know if you will photograph her tomorrow afternoon." This honour came most unexpectedly.

Next morning I got out of bed earlier than usual, shaved myself a little more carefully, put on a dark blue suit with a quiet, formal tie, and set off for the palace to make arrangements for the great occasion. It was still quite early in the morning when I arrived; flowers were being carried about in bowls, and housemaids were still busy with their dusters. Through the windows could be heard the changing of the guard—the commands of the officers shouting to their men sounded like someone retching—beyond the gardens the roar of traffic.

Although the palace is of vast size, there is no feeling of remoteness, and the hovering crowds outside seen through the windows seem uncomfortably near at hand. In my search for suitable settings the superintendent took me to the various drawing rooms, the Throne Room, and the more intimate sitting rooms of the palace. There was much to see and admire: long corridors hung with red velvet curtains; tapestries, Riesener furniture, Chinese porcelains, *objets d'art,* and, in the long and ugly gallery which has a roof like a railway station, a collection of pictures which includes Rembrandt, Van Dyke, Vermeer, and Gainsborough. During the last twenty years the Victorian additions have been carefully removed, so that today the effect of Regency and Edwardian decoration was everything that I could have hoped for. I would like to take pictures in the yellow and blue drawing rooms. I was fired with enthusiasm.

A courtier arrived to tell me that Her Majesty wished to see me about the dresses to be worn. Like all courtiers, this particular gentleman appeared to assume an air of slight stage fright at the mention of royalty and thus successfully infected me with a becoming nervousness. We looked grave, as if we were expecting news of severe illness or some other disaster, while we waited a moment outside the door of the Queen's study.

"The Queen is talking on the telephone," the courtier told me sadly, "but

King George VI

Queen Elizabeth at Buckingham.

Queen Elizabeth
and the Princesses
at Windsor

Queen Elizabeth.

The Royal Family

I'll try to get you in quickly, because, as a matter of fact, I know"—now he was imparting to me the worst news of all—"she has got the hairdresser at eleven." I felt duly appalled.

"The Queen is ready now."

Before my eyes swam a hazy impression of a room with blue silk walls embroidered with bouquets of silver-and-white flowers. Flower pictures in gold frames and real flowers everywhere—hydrangeas, sweet peas, carnations. The Queen, in pale grey, looked dazzlingly pink and white in the glaring light from the huge garden windows. She exuded a fragrance of tuberoses and gardenias as she moved towards her desk, on which stood a pot of sweet geranium.

I found myself standing very stiff, my knees shaking a bit, and blurting out with idiotic determination and unnecessary volume, "It is a great happiness for me, ma'am." I believe I even repeated this sentiment several times.

The Queen did not show her surprise, but smiled effortlessly.

"It is very exciting for me," she confided with a forlorn shake of her head. In her customary and brilliant way she put me completely at my ease, and we discussed with a certain relish the proceedings for the afternoon. I was beguiled by the slightly hesitant manner in which she spoke. It gave great point to the delayed word and created a charming atmosphere of shyness and humility.

"I thought—perhaps—I might wear—a *dress* which perhaps you *know*— with bead embroideries? Perhaps you know I wore it—in *Canada?*" At the end of each sentence the voice trailed higher in interrogation. "And then— perhaps a dress of *tulle?* Do you think? And a"—and this she said with a wistful air of apology—"a—*tiara?*"

I asked that as much jewellery as possible should be worn.

With a witty look in the eyes the Queen said, "The choice isn't very great, you know."

By now I had become bold enough to suggest perhaps also we might have a garden-party dress with a long skirt? I would like so much to take pictures outside on the lawns. I even had the temerity to suggest that, since photographic lamps are so brilliant, perhaps a rather strong "make-up" could be attempted.

"I'll try, if you really need it, but," said the Queen apologetically, "I'm not very good at it, you know."

The Queen has a genius for making every man feel she needs his protection. I knew I would have to use all my experience and ingenuity when tackling the afternoon's work, for there are certain people who are photogenic and others who are not, and I suspected that Her Majesty belonged to

The Duchess of Kent

the second class. The camera is a relentless, impersonal medium which sees everyone in its own particular way; and to the eye of a painter the photographic vision sometimes bears little resemblance to his own. I decided that, of all painters, the most suitable to express the Queen's personality would have been Renoir; that his palette could best portray the opalescent delicacies of her complexion and sympathetic warmth of the thrushlike eyes. But today there is no Renoir, and I was to face my job this afternoon with a camera.

I now watched very carefully the varying lights playing upon the Queen's face as she moved about the room. I was familiar, from millions of photographs seen in the press, with so many aspects of these features; but, of all the pictures I had ever scrutinised, only one had the Queen's charm and quality of porcelain luminosity. Taken in a hospital, Her Majesty was leaning over a child patient, with the light reflected from the bed linen, and the blush-rose effect that beguiles one's eye each time one sees her was successfully suggested. I left the palace that morning having decided to take the afternoon's pictures in reflected light.

By early afternoon there was major activity in the yellow and blue drawing rooms, where screens had been put into the semicircular bay over which were hanging my old familiar backgrounds—the Piranesi ruined arch, the Fragonard trees, the architectural vista. A mass of flowers from Windsor Castle were banked about, and an army of men were fixing lights and making various preparations. Soon I became anxious about the time they took. At any moment now the Queen might be ready. I did not wish to waste a precious minute, especially as the superintendent had told me that I would not be permitted much time with Her Majesty; that in the late King George's reign no photographer was ever allowed to take pictures for more than twenty minutes.

A hustle in the corridors, a rush of pages, and the Queen appeared in a richly encrusted crinoline of gold and silver, for which the yellow drawing room made the ideal setting. At once I started frenziedly clicking the camera. This seemed to amuse and delight Her Majesty, for from the moment I began the photographic attack on her she showed that she was enjoying herself.

In the soft light of a summer afternoon penetrating the palace windows, the Queen looked much lovelier than she had this morning. I was afraid that perhaps, when artificial light was added, the effect might not be as delicate; but suddenly, when the lamps, placed low on the Savonnerie carpets, went on in a blaze, the Queen looked even more radiant. My problems were not at all serious. For how could I fail to make entrancing pictures? The bright and sympathetically wistful eyes regarded me with an uncompromising kindliness. With the minimum of effort the mouth forms a smile which is as fresh as a dewdrop, and no creases are ever formed at its sides; the arms and wrists are white and rounded as those of an early Victorian marble statue; the hands are country hands rather than those of someone living in a city, with the fingernails cut short and mercifully without varnish; her dark hair seems to belong to another more conventional and adult woman; the appearance combines that of a child and a great lady.

After the preliminary pictures had been taken with the big camera, we walked from room to room, while en route I took more photographs with my small camera. The electricians and my assistant could never work fast enough; the sitting was progressing with such ease and rapidity that I beamed with pleasure. The Queen tidied the frills on her corsage meticulously, placed her fan so, and then prepared for the next picture to be taken. It was only when the plates had all been used and had to be reloaded in the improvised darkroom of the palace cellars that I could allow the Queen to change into another dress.

The background of the scene now passed to the blue drawing room. I refilled my Rolleiflex camera, and the Queen reappeared in white tulle spangled like a fairy doll. Rather apologetically and with a smile she admitted that she had changed the tiara. "And these diamonds—are they all right?" A tentative hand moved towards her throat and the two rows of diamonds, as big as walnuts, which the King had given as a Coronation present.

This latest apparition was even more exquisite than the last. Here I felt it necessary to apologise for my overenthusiasm, and trusted the results might warrant such an excess of zeal on my part. The Queen trusted so, too, and excused me my boorishness, but she wondered very much if the results would really come up to my expectations.

"It is so distressing to me," she continued, "that I always photograph so badly."

I complimented Her Majesty on the way she was able to look at the press cameras and cinematograph apparatus with such a candid, fearless regard.

"It isn't so difficult, you know, when there are forty of them. Then they seem to merge into one big fog of mechanism."

"And even more difficult it must be to smile naturally at the photographers."

"I find it's hard to know when *not* to smile."

One disadvantage of being a photographer is that, although many a camera session may make a great impression on the photographer's mind at the time, as soon as he has seen the results of the photography he remembers the photographs instead of his original mental vision. This was being such a happy experience that in a determined effort to remember how the Queen looked to me now I closed my eyes so that I could photograph this occasion on my brain—I would not only have the photographic interpretation of the afternoon as a souvenir. To this day in my memory I have a picture of Her Majesty standing by a Caffiéri desk in her dew-spangled dress in the yellow drawing room, with rose-flushed cheeks and star-bright eyes.

The new set of reloaded plates was used up with rapidity. The Rolleiflex did stout service whenever the big camera was not available. Pictures were taken of the Queen against the porphyry pillars of the drawing room, in the ornate doorways, sitting on gilt sofas. The superintendent, in a fit of spontaneous enthusiasm, rushed up and said, "Your Majesty, it's lovely! It's just like a Winterhalter picture." The Queen watched her reflection in the long looking glasses and was pleased with the various effects, like a pretty child in a new party dress.

Then the sun shone for the first time that day to give me new inspiration. We took many more pictures with shafts of light pouring down from the high windows onto the small figure that stood in the distance looking like an illustration of a fairy story.

Again we ran out of films. This became a joke. The Queen looked incredulously at the stock of used plates and then again at the Rolleiflex. "Is it empty again?" And when once more another roll of films was finished, she remarked, "Never have I known such celerity!"

I had already photographed the Queen in a variety of lighting arrangements and poses, and I had taken—"especially for the King"—some without a tiara, and the Queen seemed willing to carry out all further suggestions and was to put on a garden-party dress in order that, "in ten to fifteen minutes," we would meet downstairs for more photography in the garden.

The somewhat awe-struck superintendent came up and said, "Do you realise you are the most fortunate young man I've ever known? Why! You've had three hours of the Queen's time already. Do you mean to say she's gone off to change once more? Why, she hasn't had her tea yet, has she? Well, it means the poor King will have to have his tea alone. Do you realise there's a man from the Office of Works in that next room since four days? He's been waiting to see Her Majesty for two minutes about the colour of the walls to be repainted in the Throne Room."

So many accidents can suddenly arise to send one off one's equilibrium. There are days when the electric lights create a harsh effect, no matter where they are placed, when a fuse blows at just the wrong moment, when a screen is knocked over, or, worst of all, the shutter of the camera gets stuck. But none of these things happened today. It was altogether a most blessed afternoon, and in such an ebullient mood as I was in, I felt nothing could stop me.

The sky was now cloudy, though opalescent shafts of light occasionally filtered through at intervals, but just as the Queen appeared, smiling and laughing, in a gust of wind on the terrace, the sun poured down upon her. She was wearing a champagne-coloured garden-party dress, picture hat, and parasol. I ran around her in circles, snapping with my small camera as we made our way towards the lake. It was by now after six o'clock, and already the cars were waiting to take Their Majesties down to the country for the start of their summer holidays. The lawns were only fitfully splashed with sunlight; but the atmosphere was strange and timeless, and I felt this expedition to photograph by the water's edge was something out of reality.

The Queen asked me how I started to take up photography and said, "I am interested in your photographs. You have such a high standard." She asked me many questions of technique and, apropos of retouching, said, "Can you do a lot afterwards? Can you take out a whole table, for instance?"

"A table is a bit much, ma'am, but I can slice people in half."

I photographed the Queen standing in the shade of a plane tree with the sunlight filtering through the leaves, giving a charmingly luminous effect.

"How the King will laugh when I tell him you photograph me always directly against the sun. We always have to spend our time running round to face the sun for the King's snapshots." When in fact the King saw these pictures, he remarked that surely they needed three thousand people surrounding the Queen, who, so solitary in her garden-party dress, looked like an unsuccessful hostess.

Photography continued under a giant stone vase; in a summerhouse which had come originally from the Admiralty, with baroque tridents supporting the roof; on the lawns by the lake, with the façade of the earlier Buckingham House in the distance. The traffic roar continued beyond the trees, the evening light began to lose its strength, and soon the sky would become rose-coloured, as if, as the Queen said, "Piccadilly were afire every night."

We were walking by the lake when the Queen remarked upon the hard times in which we were living. "The overhanging doom—the prospect of war—is so bad for our nerves; and nowadays none of us has leisure. But history shows that periods of suffering, anxiety, and terror have produced great art, and that smug contentedness and overeating produce nothing. Perhaps we shall create something great later on, but just now I think we live in a very barren age artistically." Later she asked, "Do you like this parasol as much as I do? The handle belonged to Catherine of Russia. It's so like her

—so gold and encrusted with jewels. She used it as a stick. Do you think she would mind my using it as a parasol which is the symbol of summer and of leisure?"

This expedition to the water garden was one of the last peacetime episodes to stand out in my memory. Soon war started; nobody had peace of mind or leisure; and it was not long afterwards that the skies of London were red with fire, and the Summer Pavilion with tridents was hurt by a bomb.

The light was now too pale for my photography. We walked back to the palace, towards the tired and baffled officials who, clustering by the doors, awaited the exodus to the country. Downstairs in the circular hall I took my leave, happy in the realisation that the morrow would bring a hundred photographs—mementoes of a charming afternoon.

During the war years that followed I many times had the honour of photographing our royal family. One winter's afternoon, for instance, I was summoned to photograph the King for official portraits to be sent out by the Ministry of Information. I was having considerable difficulty in getting the lights and backgrounds arranged to my liking, and I remember I had to keep mopping my brow, for so great was my anxiety that I had begun to sweat in a most alarming manner. It was one of those nightmare occasions when everything seemed to conspire against me. I had just finished photographing His Majesty and, by no means satisfied with the pictures I had so far taken, I was about to embark upon taking "conversation pieces" of the King with his Queen and two daughters. Still the lights were in a defiant mood, and I could not dispose of the various shadows I wished, when my assistant came up to me and whispered that he now must leave me. I looked at him in amazement.

"But you cannot possibly go now! What on earth is the reason for your wanting to go?"

He replied that he had to rush back to the studio to take a photograph of a girl in a sweater for the *Pattern Book*. I went to the nearest telephone to call up the *Pattern Book* office to explain the photographer's absence. Of course they understood. I returned and explained to my assistant that he must remain with me until the sitting was over. He remained, but there was something about the manner in which he put the plates in and out of the camera which showed me that his enthusiasm for the job of photographing the royal family was not occupying his undivided attention, and I knew that he had half his mind on the girl in the sweater.

Later during the same evening an even more humiliating occurrence befell me. The sitting, which had gone so "stickily" at first, was, after four hours' work, beginning to take on a life of its own, and a few charming unforeseen effects were gifts to raise my battered spirits. Suddenly a page appeared with a piece of paper on a silver tray.

The King stepped forward. "Is that for me?"

"No, Your Majesty. It is a note left for Mr. Beaton."

I read a message from the lady driver from the Ministry of Information who was to dash with these pictures to the attendant developer at West Ealing. She had written:

"Am tired of waiting outside for package. Have gone home for the night."

One evening during the war, Hugh Francis, my boss at the Ministry of Information, telephoned to say that a very important visitor was expected on the morrow and would be staying at Buckingham Palace. For security reasons I must not ask his or her name. But would I please be at the palace in the afternoon prepared to take a photograph of this visitor with the royal family? I was extremely curious to know who this V.I.P. might be and wondered if perhaps President Roosevelt was flying to this country for a conference. When next day I arrived at the palace the unknown arrival was still referred to as "our guest." Later, however, I learned that the visitor was to be the wife of the President, Mrs. Roosevelt.

In consequence of the recent bombing of the palace, most of the living rooms had been dismantled, the porcelain and china ornaments taken from the cupboards, and the more valuable pictures removed from the walls. The room in which the photographic groups were to be taken was empty of everything except a few chairs and sofas, and I thought to give an impression of this emptiness and discomfort in which Their Majesties were living. The lights were set up and trained upon a corner of a living room which showed a cupboard bereft of ornaments and only a few pieces of furniture around. Various secretaries and equerries came in with the latest reports of Mrs. Roosevelt's arrival.

"The airplane has touched down."

"She has now stepped into a train."

"The train will arrive at Paddington in five minutes."

"The train has arrived."

"Mrs. Roosevelt has been received by the King and Queen."

"Mrs. Roosevelt is now on her way to the palace."

"Mrs. Roosevelt had gone up to her room."

The King and Queen with the Princesses came in to see the scene I had decided to depict. His Majesty, looking into the ground glass of the camera, observed, "I see you're getting in that empty cupboard. Is that a good idea?" Instead of admitting that the point of showing its emptiness was to give an indication of the way the family lived at this time, I lied and said that I thought the shadows cast by the yellow marble columns would hide the emptiness of the cupboard.

"Mrs. Roosevelt is on her way downstairs."

"Mrs. Roosevelt is coming along the corridor."

"Mrs. Roosevelt!"

Mrs. Roosevelt joined Their Majesties for tea, and ten minutes later the family party came in to be photographed. Mrs. Roosevelt, impressively tall, smiling in a circulating manner, loped in with the long-legged walk of a colt. I was presented to her, but she did not seem to see me and appeared extremely vague about what was happening. Only when the lights were switched on did she seem to realise that pictures were about to be taken.

The group formed itself on sofas, chairs, and stools in front of the empty cupboard. I placed Mrs. Roosevelt's feet—so. She looked somewhat surprised at this attention, and I realised I had done something silly. Mrs. Roosevelt does not come under the same category as most of my photographic subjects. In life she exudes such a magnanimous quality of bigheartedness and lack of pettiness that it is quite beside the point to try to make her into a good-looking woman. She is a woman with distinction, integrity, and charm, and as such she is complete. She rises above the usual level of criticism. It does not matter if she wears an idiotic hat; she does not believe in that hat herself; it is only a token. It is equally silly to arrange her feet just so.

I felt very like a Victorian photographer when, amid this barrage of lights, I shouted instructions to my illustrious sitters to remain still for one full second. I guessed it would strike Mrs. Roosevelt, coming from America, and accompanied almost wherever she goes by a storm of flash bulbs, that England was very behindhand if its royal photographer had to shout, "One, two, three —go." But I had not reckoned that Mrs. Roosevelt could not hear my instructions. The noise of the engines of the transatlantic airplane was still buzzing in her ears, and she was deaf to my entreaties not to move. I daresay, too, Mrs. Roosevelt considered that she was being photographed by a moving-picture camera for the newsreels; and so, as she sat between the King and Queen, she turned her head this way, then that, smiling, nodding, thrusting her head backwards, and giving a fine display, while the young Princesses looked on with a certain amusement and I was unable to catch a successful time exposure.

When later I showed the photographs to Her Majesty and confessed my feelings of stupidity at having to ask for one second's stillness, the Queen sympathised with me by saying, "I must say, Mrs. Roosevelt showed great mobility." When the King saw the photographs he remarked, "I knew from that vantage point the empty cupboard would show."

Sometimes before a royal sitting I am granted an audience at which the preparations for the proposed sitting are discussed. Not yet burdened by the responsibility of the camera and equipment, I am free to look around and talk freely. Although the camera may bring me face to face with the person I most wish to converse with, during the photographic session itself I have little time. The process of taking photographs, especially with a big camera, needs acute concentration; and much as I should enjoy being able to keep up a running conversation, it is quite impossible to talk and to watch at the same time every detail of what's happening in front of the lens. There is so much to notice: whether or not a candlestick in the background is protruding from my sitter's nose *en profil;* if the line of the cheek is clear; if the fingers have wriggled themselves into a ball of worms or are looking like a bundle of asparagus. It is difficult for me to give instructions and to ask or answer questions; and when the whole sitting is over, although there are a few moments for chat and an exchange of *politesse,* I am always reminded of lingering by the dentist's door when, for the first time, the patient smiles with a sense of relief and the knowledge that escape is now at hand.

Once during the war Sir Eric Miéville telephoned to say there was a question of my photographing Princess Elizabeth in honour of her attaining her majority, and the Queen would be graciously pleased to see me at six o'clock on the next Monday evening.

It was during one of the interminably long winters towards the end of the war. It had been a day of rain, slush, and dirt for me working for the Ministry of Information in the East End of London. There was an early blackout, no taxis, and I had to rush home to change my clothes. The house was cold, and no servant was in to answer my shouts of despair as I rushed through the front door on my way to my bedroom.

"Where are my shirts? Where are my shoes? Where is my blue suit?"

I bellowed like a mad bull as I threw every sort of unwanted garment through the air. I was giving vent to the most vociferous display of despairing self-pity, when my mother suddenly appeared. She had been deep in some historical romance and had not yet surfaced to contemporary reality.

"What on earth is happening?" she enquired, looking very baffled. "What on earth is this noise?"

I explained my frantic predicament. My mother came to the rescue.

"I do see you can't keep the Queen waiting," she said. "But isn't this the suit you want hanging up here?"

She polished my shoes for me on my feet as I put on a clean shirt and tied my tie.

Down the stairs three at a time. Bang! The front door shut. I raced along the streets. Still no taxis. The Underground was slower than ever; but in spite of a sudden rainstorm I miraculously managed to get a taxi at Hyde Park Corner and arrived with palpitating heart at the palace with five minutes to spare.

I was shown into Her Majesty's sitting room. Cascades of spider chrysanthemums, a Richard Wilson on an easel, with a large Paul Nash propped beneath; early Victorian pictures on the brocade walls, a mass of photographs of the family, and books. The room had the peace of a room in the country. From the book left on the arm of an easy chair, it seemed that the Queen was reading a biography of Cézanne.

After listening to the six o'clock news on the radio Her Majesty came in exuding serenity. Hers is a wonderful quality; nothing seems to fluster her. We sat down to talk, and it transpired that I was to take pictures of the whole family and afterwards some special ones of Princess Elizabeth. I asked if, since we had taken many sittings here in Buckingham Palace, we could not take the new pictures at Windsor.

"May I ask the King if that would be all right?"

Dresses were discussed. Why were men so much better at designing than women? I told Her Majesty of my projected visit to the Far East. "Oh, the thrill of leaving this lovely, gloomy island! There is no colour here in wartime; everything dark khaki, but enlivened by the wonderful English spirit!" I remarked that the war news was now so good that perhaps while I was away the war might be over and I would regret so much not being outside to cheer Her Majesty onto the balcony.

"The balcony, since the bombing, isn't really safe."

"But, ma'am, shouldn't it be reinforced at once?"

"Wouldn't that be courting a setback? Perhaps we'd better have all the materials ready standing by; the cement and stones piled in a corner."

Four days later Sir Eric Miéville telephoned to say the Queen was expecting me to take photographs of the family at Windsor Castle on the Monday morning; I should be there at eleven to take the Princesses, and the King and Queen would be available in the afternoon. In the face of the usual difficulties, this meant a rush for the arrangements, for even in wartime it seems many people are away on Saturday. However, early on a wet and foggy morning we started off in a palace car and collected a new background—an enlargement of a "Velvet" Brueghel—in Ealing on our way.

Windsor Castle, vast and cold. The family were now living around the courtyard in rooms built by George IV which had Gothic additions. There was a van delivering coal at the entrance at which we should have arrived, so I was taken to the service entrance and got an interesting glimpse of the vast underworld of scullion maids filling ancient-looking water bottles and creating an almost medieval effect of bustle. A sergeant telephoned to announce my arrival to the lady in waiting. He was calm and jocose, saying into the mouthpiece to some friend, "Oh! I didn't recognise your voice; I thought it was some gentleman speaking."

We wandered for miles down long corridors to the lady in waiting's sitting room. A very small fire was burning in the grate. Victorian chintz, radio, a historical novel. The room was empty.

The corridors had been stripped of most of their ornaments. Queen Mary's collection of miniatures had been hidden from bombs. The passages were icy-cold. We passed rooms where a few token flowers had been arranged in vases, but at this time of the year there was nothing but leathery chrysanthemums. We walked past offices with scarlet leather boxes on the tables, and I could detect the distant smell of a cigar. At last we found the lady in waiting trying to find me—Lady Hyde, in maroon wool. Her Majesty apologised that there was no equerry to look after me; they were all out shooting with His Majesty but would be back for luncheon.

After enjoying the warming effects of a glass of sherry I started to get the electric lights rigged up—a full-scale operation—and the equipment of wires and gadgets looked like a film studio. The state rooms, magnificently ornate with brocade on the walls and a wealth of gilt, have tremendous doors which did not seem to keep out draughts. There had been no fires lit in the grates since last year, and the cold was such that one's breath came out in clouds of white steam. I chose various rooms for the pictures, and soon the Princesses appeared on the Gothic landing which I had thought would make a fairy-story-like setting for the first pictures.

The Princesses were very agreeable and comported themselves through a long day's photography with tact, patience, and a certain subdued gaiety. I remember thinking how much Princess Elizabeth had grown, that she was still schoolgirlish and apt to look heavy in repose, but that when her face lit up into a smile she was utterly delightful. Princess Elizabeth has the same hesitancy of speech and the gift for the *mot juste* as her mother, though I noticed that when the Queen was present her daughter made no conversational effort and lapsed into silence.

The Queen, wearing a banana-coloured dress with a cape of fox fur, made the day exceedingly pleasant for me. She seemed to think it great fun to photograph the Windsor-Gothic staircase, and wandered about exuding a feeling of leisure and enjoyment.

Luncheon was ordered for one-thirty—"then we will take pictures afterwards." There was quite a party lined up in front of the fire, including the

French governess, Sir Piers Legh, Sir Ulick Alexander, and Gerald Kelly, the Royal Academician, who, it seems, had been in the castle painting one picture after another for the last four years. The royal family reappeared; the King was wearing tweeds, which looked incongruous in these gilded rooms and because one had grown accustomed to seeing His Majesty in uniform during these war years. Deep bows and curtsies from the household. We trooped into luncheon. I was proud to be placed on the Queen's right and delighted to find conversation so easy.

The luncheon was good, and, refreshed, I returned to the photographic fray; but I succeeded only partially in getting the family into interesting groups. I found it difficult to make unconventional compositions, for, so often has this family been photographed in formal attitudes, that it is almost impossible to break down the results of their training to stand in line. But, in all, I felt my day was successful. The King was in good spirits and looked extremely handsome, like a carved wooden effigy, in the naval uniform into which he had now changed. We took pictures in colour and exposed altogether a great number of plates before Their Majesties had to go back to London.

The Queen wistfully shook her head. "Perhaps you would do some more pictures in the summer when we could wear pretty clothes? And perhaps the war will be . . . ?"

The Princesses ran up to rehearse their pantomime, and I motored back to London in the black-out.

The results of the photographs of Princess Elizabeth were not as charming as the occasion warranted. Somehow I had not been able to get the lights under my control, and hard shadows appeared where I did not want them. I had tried to make every possible readjustment, but a photographer cannot battle for too long with the lights while his sitter waits and loses confidence. I knew at the time I was taking pictures of which I would not be proud, yet there was no alternative. The background looked fussy; as it was wartime, the setting of the pictures should be simple and unostentatious. When the pictures appeared on Her Royal Highness's birthday I felt I had not proved myself worthy of the high honour conferred on me.

Some three years later, however, I was able to justify myself. I was fortunate enough to be allowed another opportunity of photographing the Princess on her "coming of age." Before the sitting I was bidden to the palace to see the Princess's dresses, which were hung for display around the walls of her bedroom. Of all that we photographed that afternoon, by far the most successful was the pink-spangled crinoline which was one of her mother's prewar dresses, now altered to fit the daughter. These sunny smiling photographs, taken against my old Fragonard background, had an enormous success and were quite the most charming that I had yet seen of the Princess.

Princess Elizabeth's easy charm, like her mother's, does not carry across in her photographs, and each time one sees her one is delighted to find how much more serene, magnetic, and at the same time meltingly sympathetic she is than one had imagined. In the photographs there is a certain heaviness which is not there in real life, and one misses, even in colour photographs, the effect of the dazzlingly fresh complexion, the clear regard from the glass-blue eyes, and the gentle, all-pervading sweetness of her smile.

Princess Margaret, however, is infinitely more photogenic and becomes increasingly so as the years bring her nearer to maturity. The first time I photographed her she was no more than a bright little child in a long party dress whom I had portrayed with her sister in a Gainsborough-like setting. During the war I photographed her on several occasions, once on the day before she had her appendix removed, which did not give me much opportunity to show her at her best. Recently, to celebrate her nineteenth birthday, more pictures were taken, and I found that she had acquired a great deal of her mother's qualities, the straight line from the nape of the neck to the small of her back, the delicate hands and wrists, and, in the old-fashioned tulle dresses, the apotheosis of all children's party dresses, she radiates her mother's aura of grace and femininity.

When photographing Princess Margaret I was conscious of how amused Her Royal Highness was by my antics during the session. I knew what a strange performance she considered me to be putting on, and I only wished for opportunities of sharing the joke. But time spent in conversation at a sitting is time in which no photographs are taken; and, since the sitting must ultimately be judged by results, the greater the number to choose from, the higher the standard of the pictures chosen is likely to be.

Later Princess Margaret related how I had asked her to put on a certain dress which a mutual friend had admired so much, but when she returned wearing the dress I had said, "Oh yes, ma'am! That will be very good for a head." "That," added Princess Margaret, "was snubs to me, snubs to the mutual friend, and snubs to my dressmaker."

When the birth of a son and heir to Princess Elizabeth and the Duke of Edinburgh was announced, the world waited expectantly for the first photograph of the child who might one day be King of England. For weeks on end press photographers with telescopic lenses attached to their cameras were stationed on the roofs of houses overlooking the gardens of Buckingham Palace, in the hopes of being able, through the bare branches of the winter trees, to catch the first glimpse of the infant being taken for an airing. But they were not successful. After two weeks a blurred picture of a nurse wheeling a perambulator was all they could produce. As the days passed and still no pictures had been taken, some portions of the press, considering it their right to have pictures of Prince Charles, became so angry that they spread erroneous reports that the child was delicate. But had not the royal family every right to decide themselves when they wished the newborn to face the penalties of public fame and submit him to a barrage of strong lights for the first time?

A few days before I was to sail for America intimation came from the palace that I might be asked to take a new sitting of Her Majesty the Queen; nothing definite could yet be arranged. I had long since wished to make photographs of the Queen in complete contrast to those taken before the war, when Her Majesty was revealed in shafts of sunlight in bouffant dresses of thistledown delicacy. I had suggested that a black velvet crinoline might make a great effect, with crimson curtains festooned around a column in a somewhat Regency atmosphere. I conferred with Norman Hartnell, the Queen's dressmaker, who at length wrote me that he had made the black velvet dress as suggested. I awaited the occasion impatiently. Time was important; I was particularly anxious to take my pictures before leaving the country—on my return spring would have arrived and the sombre colours of my portrait would appear less suitable.

Early on the morning of the day tentatively fixed for my summons to the palace the Queen's secretary telephoned. "I'm afraid I'm interrupting your breakfast," he said, "but I wanted to contact you early, as Her Majesty would like you to come along as soon as possible to take pictures of her. And then Her Majesty wondered if you would like to take some pictures of the young Prince; but, as he has his lunch at twelve-thirty, there wouldn't be much time."

My heart missed several beats. I shaved so quickly that I gashed my chin. I put on an evening shirt under my blue suit, as it happened to be the only one I had near me, and made frantic, almost incoherent, telephone calls; but within an hour the lights and my new painted backgrounds were installed in the music room at the palace.

I stood about waiting and making desultory conversation and realised I was much more nervous than ever before. Her Majesty appeared in the black velvet crinoline with tiara and diamonds like robin's eggs around her throat. The effect was spectacular. Though entirely different from her aspect before the war, the Queen's appearance in severe black velvet was every bit as successful. Photographs were taken in many different portions of the palace, and my old painted backgrounds, by contrast to the furnishings of the Throne Room and various drawing rooms, appeared extremely shabby. But, in fact, the pictures taken against the coarse painted backings proved the most successful.

So pleasant was the experience that, as usual, the sitting took much longer than the time allotted; and I was too late to photograph Prince Charles before his midday meal.

Would I like to come back early in the afternoon, or would I like to stay and have luncheon at the palace? Her Majesty enquired. There were so many complicated arrangements to be made for getting the photographs processed and distributed before I left the country that I felt I must hurry back to my house and start putting things in motion. Running out of the palace courtyard, I began hailing occupied taxis. There are few worse centres in London for finding an empty taxi than outside Buckingham Palace.

When I eventually reached home, the moment my foot was inside the hall I was plunged into pandemonium. My secretary, Maud Nelson, was at the telephone, lifting the receiver, saying, "No, sorry!" and putting it down again. At once another ring. "No, sorry!" and so it had continued for one hour past. Dorothy, the maid, was out of breath from running up and down stairs, answering doorbells. The press, by some mysterious process, had got wind of the fact that I was photographing Prince Charles. Could they have the pictures? Could the Wilmington *Gazette* have an exclusive photograph of Prince Charles? Could *Life* send a photographer to take a picture of Mr. Beaton leaving the palace? Could the *Star* send a journalist to interview Mr. Beaton? "No, sorry!" "No, sorry!"

There is something exciting but sinister about having the press on your track, and I felt suddenly as hounded as if I had committed a murder. When it was time for me to return to the palace I ducked out of the front door past a group of waiting journalists and into a hired car. Back among my assistants, electricians, and property men at the palace, I awaited the child's appearance. I had colour films, big cameras, small cameras, a battery of lights, and a good deal of daylight filtered through the large windows from the wintry scene outside.

A pink chiffon-and-lace cot was wheeled in by Princess Elizabeth's maid, and we admired the filigree work of the lace and the small heart-shaped cushion. Every detail of this cot belonged to a Lilliputian world. The cushion for the Prince's head was the size of a large biscuit, and the bunches of baby ribbon were in miniature. Suddenly it dawned upon me that my sitter this afternoon was to be on a quite different scale from the sitters to whom I was accustomed. I must train the lights down onto a smaller radius, must close in my effects.

The Princess, with wild-rose complexion, periwinkle-blue eyes, and a cool refreshing smile, came in, followed by her nurse holding the precious bundle. Bows left and right. My assistants presented in turn; and an awed silence descended as we all, electricians, assistants, and property boys alike, took our first look at the baby whose large blue eyes surveyed the world about him with such wonder. I was astonished that a three-week-old baby should already have so much character, and I felt that the child already bore some resemblance to his grandmother and great-uncle. For so young a child he seemed to have a remarkable range of expression; and I was fascinated by the looks of surprise, disdain, defiance, anger, and delight that ran across his minute face. The little fingers were remarkably long and pointed.

So serene was his mood that we must not delay. The Prince was placed in the pink cot; a light was trained down onto the back of the little head, bathing the face in a glow of reflected light; and as the wide-open eyes gazed into my Rolleiflex, the lens opened and shut, and the first photograph of Prince Charles had been taken. In fact, this photograph was considered the best of the sitting, and one chosen for world-wide publication. From that moment I continued to snap, while Prince Charles regulated a variety of happy moods. His mother sat by the cot and, holding his hand, watched his gyrations with curiosity, pride, and amusement.

The afternoon passed agreeably but quickly. Soon the windows let in very little daylight, and we had to rely on the battery of standard lights for our effects. I photographed mother and son together in numberless different poses and, when the child had a bout of restlessness, Princess Elizabeth posed alone. I took many charming pictures of her in colour against the grisaille background of a landscape by Patinir, wearing a slate-blue dress, the only colour in the picture being provided by her pink cheeks and lips.

I was eager to take even more photographs; but by now the child had grown tired and restive, and there was nothing for me but to wait with the camera ready to click at any lucky moment. Thus I was able to get many remarkable action pictures, but the best of the afternoon was over, and the Prince began to cry noisily. I enjoyed the contrast between the splendour of these rooms, with their gilt-and-blue porphyry columns, and the natural simplicity of mother, child, and nurse. The child would cry or gurgle, would burst out laughing or put out his tongue; the mother would turn him from one shoulder to another, lift him above her head to admire him once again,

2 1 0

until the nurse finally took control, brought the baby to within a few feet of the glowing fires, rearranged the safety pins, and returned to his mother a calmer, sleepier infant.

Daylight had disappeared by the time the long sitting was at an end, and I delivered my negatives to the developer. When I returned to my house the onslaught of the press had become yet more intense, and my secretary, knowing there would be no peace at home, had arranged for me to stay with a friend.

By working on the films all night, my assistants were able to produce pictures next day; and we were delighted to find that there were dozens of extraordinarily successful pictures. One which particularly pleased us was the first picture of the sitting, the picture that showed the Prince looking wide-eyed at the world. Confident of success, I took the photographs to Buckingham Palace. Princess Elizabeth scrutinised them with a loving care and admitted she was very pleased. Four of her favourites were passed for publication; and, proud of having brought off a great coup, leaving the problems of coping with the press to my secretary, I sailed for America.

There are quite definite and strict rules relating to the publication of all photographs emanating from the palace. No one paper or magazine may have any picture exclusively, the photographer must sell his pictures at stipulated rates, and no one can be given preference. Everyone is given a fair chance, and there is no excuse for breaking the rules. The press department of the palace set a certain date for the publication of my pictures of Prince Charles; they were not to be released before the official group pictures of the christening. Nevertheless, during the next few weeks my secretary was driven almost hysterical by the press's repeated requests that she help them break the embargo. Even during the small hours of the morning, in my New York hotel, some editor would telephone me from Canada, suggesting that, as a paper in Norway had already published the pictures, I should give my permission for the others to be released forthwith. I felt, however, that I was in possession of a precious heirloom which must be carefully guarded.

When in England the *Evening Standard* reprinted my picture, published, contrary to every stipulation, by the French *Paris Soir,* and the embargo was finally broken, all hell was let loose in Fleet Street, and I was glad to be out of the country. Some newspapers wrote exceedingly discourteous articles about me, and an evening paper reported, quite erroneously, that I had made a large sum of money by selling the pictures to America. Much as I had appreciated the honour of being the first to photograph the newborn Prince, I incurred many penalties; and I learned with regret that, if you possess something the gentlemen of the press wish to have, there is usually no gainsaying them.

During the summer months of 1950, when the British press informed us that Princess Elizabeth was expecting another child, and at last when that child, a daughter, was born, there was speculation as to which photographer would be allowed to take the first pictures. The telephone at my house would ring at the most unexpected times of day and night, and some impatient sub-editor would enquire if I could tell him exactly when I should be able to supply him with photographs, as he wished to make his plans accordingly. The reply that I could not tell him was usually received with distrust and a certain animosity.

In the past I had relied upon the Queen making a spontaneous suggestion that I should be sent for with my camera to document some event. But the King and Queen were at Balmoral. I thought, perhaps, it would not be considered too presumptuous if I wrote to Martin Charteris, Princess Elizabeth's private secretary, asking if I might have the honour of taking the first photographs of Princess Anne, as those I had taken of Prince Charles had been considered successful. My note received an encouraging reply, and when the child was one month old I was summoned to Clarence House.

For almost two months on end England had suffered from appalling weather. September proved as big a disappointment as August; in the country the crops were rotting in the fields under pouring rain; in London the skies were so lowering that daylight photography was almost out of the question. I had been asked to bring as little equipment as possible for the sitting, so I depended a great deal on the day. On the thirteenth of September, the day before my session, the rain poured like rods from a slate sky. I was not perturbed, for I have of late become increasingly superstitious, and fourteen is for me a lucky number. I felt confident that all would go well; so indeed it turned out.

I had an agreeable luncheon at the Ritz Hotel, given to celebrate the opening of an exhibition of paintings done by one of my friends. As we sat at a table by the windows looking on to the Park, the sun poured down on our party with such unaccustomed brilliance that one of the ladies asked if the awnings could be lowered. I left the luncheon party early for a two-fifteen appointment and walked rather jauntily through the park on my way to Clarence House; for, as I looked up between the dark green of the overhanging branches, the sky was clear and blue.

Martin Charteris showed me a number of pale-coloured rooms in the Princess's house, in case some corner should present itself as being more suited to photographic purposes than the Princess's sitting room, which had been suggested as the scene for the afternoon's activity. Indeed there were many opportunities for charming photographs in the white-and-gold drawing room (although most of the furniture was hidden under dust covers), in the ground-floor sitting rooms looking on to the garden, the long hall corridor with columns—columns are always a great asset, and almost every view is flattered when framed by them—or even the dining room with its pale green walls and ancestor portraits framed in white stucco decoration.

But perhaps, after all, the sitting room possessed most advantage. Two sides of the room consisted almost entirely of windows; through their net curtains the sun filtered in a becoming diffusion; the duck-egg blue of the remaining walls, the pale curtains and carpet would not eat up light. In fact, so strong was the general illumination in here that we could take instantaneous pictures—an enormous advantage, of course, when photographing any subject as elusive as children. Moreover, this room had an air of being lived in; the sofas and chairs were covered with chintz; on the walls hung portraits of Princess Elizabeth and Prince Philip; a large highly polished Panatrope radio-gramophone stood cater-cornered; there were bronze and gold chrysanthemums in cut-glass vases and over the fireplace, on the many small tables, on the shelves of the Chippendale bookcase, and on the large useful-looking desk was arrayed, in traditional royal taste, a miscellaneous display of family snapshots and photographs. On the sofa a number of lace pillows and shawls and coverlets had been placed.

We were busy seeking out odd corners for camera angles when Prince Charles (now aged nearly two), in a blue suit, came rushing into the room, holding by the hand a housemaid he had discovered on his way from the nursery. He had become a most sturdy little chap since the last time I had photographed him, with rather heavy pink cheeks, his eyes starlike, his pale gold hair as silken as only a child's hair can be. He had just started to talk. "Baby here?" he asked. "No, no baby yet." He was gone from the room in a flash. A few moments later Miss Lightbody, the chief nurse, came in with Prince Charles, and Sister Rowe followed, bearing in her arms the Princess Anne—a small baby with quite a definite nose for one so young, large sleepy grey-green eyes, and a particularly pretty mouth, with the upper lip curving to an almost exaggerated rosebud.

Sister Rowe warned me, "You'd better hurry if you want to get her with her eyes open, as she is already very sleepy."

"Not a moment to be lost! Hurry, boys!" I instructed my assistants. We closed in upon the infant as she lay in Sister's arms by the window. But Sister sat with her back to the garden, keeping out most of the light from the

Prince Charles.
The first photograph.

Prince Charles
and Princess Anne

baby, who was already preparing to settle down for a comfortable afternoon's nap.

"This won't do!" Before we were able to readjust the scene, Princess Elizabeth, in a pistachio-checked dress, appeared, and she seemed very amused by the spectacle confronting her of so many grown-up people doing —apart from using their fingers—everything in their power to keep the baby's eyes open; bird noises were made, shouts let off unexpectedly, hands clapped together, keys jangled. Three Rolleiflexes were suddenly put to great use, and another, filled with colour film, was at hand for a picture if the opportunity arose.

Sometimes I feel the responsibility of the occasion weighs heavily on me; I am full of nervous apprehensions. But this afternoon, although I felt sure that I was taking a great number of very bad photographs, I was infected nevertheless by the prevalent mood of gaiety. Everyone seemed to be in excellent spirits; the nurse and sister in fine fettle, my assistants obviously enjoying themselves, and Princess Elizabeth herself often bending backwards with a sudden jolt of laughter at some unexpected happening. The only person who was not rising to the occasion was the little Princess Anne herself.

Babies are difficult to photograph at the best of times, but if a baby is in a fretful mood and is longing to be allowed to sleep, it is almost impossible to persuade it into a change of mood. But, considering that Princess Anne was obviously in no mind to enjoy her first photographic sitting, we were extremely fortunate. I continued the afternoon's work for some time before I asked Princess Elizabeth if I was trespassing too long on her good nature. But it is typical of Princess Elizabeth that she wished to continue with the work long after the novelty and the element of amusement had worn off; a job had to be done and results must be achieved. Princess Elizabeth stood with the child by a window, sat on a sofa, on a chair, moved from one corner of the room to another, and was a monument of serenity and patience.

"Put her on this arm, Sister. I think this arm would be happier."

Princess Elizabeth has a voice of bell-like clarity which possesses the pathos of a child; and she has her mother's instinct for choosing her words with care and seldom uses the stock phrase.

Sister Rowe produced a small bottle of glycerine and, using her finger as a stopper, turned it upside down. Then she put a drop on the baby's tongue. The little Princess quite suddenly passed into a tranquil mood, and for a few minutes we were able to photograph her as she gazed out on this new world with surprise. It struck me that this child, like Prince Charles nearly two years ago, showed an extraordinary variety of expression for one so young.

The afternoon's excitement infected Prince Charles, who was anxious to be in the centre of so much activity and kept touching his sister with his podgy, dimpled hands. Prince Charles was at the stage when he was interested in everything; a live wire, he never flagged in energy, even when those around him were exhausted. One minute he was up on a window sill, giving an unexpected treat to the passers-by below, pulling at the curtain cords; the next he was climbing onto the sofa to take the cigarettes out of a silver box; then he would be absorbed with interest in the working of his mother's snapshot camera. He would imitate our strange cries to the baby, and he showed such interest in our efforts to photograph her that he would occasionally join our subject, and at one moment—it reminded me of the great moment in the *Sleeping Beauty* ballet—he kissed the baby on her cheek, and I was able to get the best picture of the afternoon.

The infant Princess had lasted out a long series of disturbances extremely well, but now at last she became thoroughly exasperated. Prince Charles, too, was getting beyond control, and the volume of noise produced by the two children was quite earsplitting. I was too tenacious, however, to be altogether lenient, and begged that we should be allowed to go down to the garden to take some pictures by the columns, through which the beds of salmon-pink geraniums and other vividly coloured flowers would make the sort of setting in which many people would like to see their Princess.

The scene in the garden became very chaotic, and at one moment I gave up any attempt at photography while I looked around. Prince Charles was rushing about the lawns wearing a policeman's helmet, which he had found in the sentry's office; corgi dogs were barking and running in circles; my assistants were putting light metres up to one another's faces or against columns. Princess Elizabeth was looking about her in a mood of quiet amazement. I made one last attempt to organise another batch of pictures, and I felt that some of the mother holding her newborn against a background of the sunlit garden should be quite successful. But at last the time had come to call a halt. Prince Charles rushed to a waiting car to go off with a nurse for his too-long-delayed afternoon's jaunt, and Princess Anne sank into Sister Rowe's arms for wonderful oblivion.

In the hall of Clarence House, Princess Elizabeth bid me good-bye and asked how soon any results might be seen. In a rash moment I promised that the pictures would be ready on the morrow. I was invited to bring the prints to show her at three o'clock. I then retired along the corridors to the household offices and made telephone calls to arrange that my promise should be fulfilled. The processing would be done right away. If I came along to the studio at seven o'clock that evening, I was told, I could see the rough prints, and from them decide which the men should enlarge during the night.

When later that evening I saw the entire batch of black-and-white photographs I was at first somewhat dismayed. In so many Princess Anne was looking angry or bored; in so many she had been caught in the abandon of a yawn. But on closer scrutiny I discovered about ten pictures that really seemed quite enchanting; and one in particular, of Prince Charles kissing his sister, was an exquisite picture of which I was proud.

Next day at three o'clock punctually Princess Elizabeth asked, "Have we been successful?" I thought I could safely say that we had been.

I pulled a small table out from against a wall, placed it by the window, and Princess Elizabeth sat at it to scrutinise the huge batch of big and small prints I had brought.

I had previously placed the enlargements in an order which I thought would be dramatically effective. I planned to show first a good one to create a comfortable impression, then, when confidence was gained, to show the less good, leaving the best, as children reserve the best spoonfuls, for the last. But suddenly I changed my mind and said, "Shall I show the best one first?" and at once placed before the Princess my favourite.

"Yes, it is delicious!" The Princess was wrapt in smiles as she looked at the picture of Prince Charles greeting his sister with a kiss and I am sure she did not hear my idiotic eulogies about the quality of its light, its composition, Prince Charles's eyelashes, and the beauty of children's hair.

"Yes, it is most fortunate in every way."

The Princess examined carefully the rest of the batch of small pictures, and a few extra were chosen to be subsequently enlarged. One picture was selected to become crown property, another to be given exclusively to the King George's Jubilee Trust, and others were chosen for release to the press, to appear just as soon as possible. I am glad to say that the Princess's choices were the same as mine.

"Thank you, ma'am. Then these will appear in the papers tomorrow morning."

"Can they really get them out so soon?" The Princess looked at me incredulously.

A very great effort is needed on all sides to distribute pictures at short notice in a way that allows everyone an equal share. But Colonel Butler of the Associated Press was only awaiting the word "Go" from me before putting into motion his vast organisation, which, in an incredibly short time, supplies pictures to the entire world. I telephoned from Clarence House giving him the code numbers of those which were passed for publication, and when I returned home the telephone bell seldom ceased pealing with enquiries from the press; a particularly tenacious reporter from a particularly mischievous morning paper was particularly lacking in sensitiveness.

I motored that evening to my house in the country, and when next morning I was called with breakfast, I saw my work on the front pages of the newspapers—"The Pictures You Have Waited to See," "First Photographs" —and was gratified to find how clearly they had been reproduced. A few moments later Colonel Butler telephoned to me from London. "The pictures are in New York already; they'll be making the evening editions; and as for the reception the pictures have had in England, why, we must congratulate ourselves!" he said. "So far there haven't been any complaints from the press! And I want you to know that one man at the office said his wife had been so thrilled when she saw the kissing picture that she couldn't eat any breakfast."

The most recent photographs I have taken of the Queen were to be used in connection with the celebration of her fiftieth birthday; and once again Her Majesty consented to give up several hours to the sitting. After I sent about two dozen of the finished proofs to the Queen's private secretary, he telephoned to tell me that Her Majesty had seen the pictures, liked them extremely well, but considered I had been perhaps a little too kind. Her Majesty felt that, since she had battered her way through a number of years, she could not have come through completely unscathed. Would it be possible at this stage to take away the retouching? This is the first time that any of my sitters has suggested that the pictures were too flattering, and it shows another facet of the remarkable character of the woman seated on the pinnacle of the throne, but with her feet so firmly planted in the earth.

Chapter 11 STAGE PHOTOGRAPHY: PUBLICITY AND MISHAPS

DURING my early passion for the Russian ballet I used to take my No. 3A Folding Pocket Kodak with me to the theatre, and at some particularly wonderful moment hold it towards the stage and press the cable release. So strong was my determination to catch the scene in front of me on the negative that I felt sure some results would appear; but I was never able to capture even the faintest blur of an image of the *Sylphides,* or *Good-Humoured Ladies.* Since early childhood my longing to take theatre pictures with my own camera had remained; and it was therefore with a sensation of victory at last that, as a professional photographer, I stepped into the magic stage world.

Of all the purposes I have put it to, I find that my Rolleiflex is perhaps best suited to theatre photography. With the usual stage lighting one can get results of great depth of focus by employing one second's exposure; and the camera is so conveniently light that one can portray an entire stage production from many different angles. It is also an expeditious method of photographing a play; for most stage sittings, if they are to be comprehensive, must last three or four exhausting hours.

Photographing stage plays is one of the aspects of my camera career that I enjoy the most, but I am conscious of its dangers. So many people's feelings are involved, and, if in the enthusiasm of a moment one happens to concentrate too much on any particular character in the play, a "situation" is likely to arise. One thing I have learned. However tired an actor may complain of being at the time of the photo call (and this is generally arranged to take place after a series of gruelling dress rehearsals), he will be extremely put out if you take compassion on him and allow him to go home. The only actor I have ever met who has felt he has been photographed too often is John Gielgud.

Gielgud, whose greatness is today generally underestimated in favour of showier stage performers with film followings, becomes extremely self-conscious at the sight of a camera, and for him the procedure of being photographed is an ordeal. Gielgud's wonderful modesty is only one of the rare qualities that this artist of integrity possesses to such a degree that he is undoubtedly, and will eventually be recognised as, "our first player." Of all the plays I have photographed, John Gielgud's production of Congreve's *Love for Love* provided the most successful pictures, for Rex Whistler's beautiful sets made convincing backgrounds for exquisite "conversation pieces."

When I designed the scenery and costumes for a revival of *Lady Windermere's Fan,* both here and on Boardway, I was so happy in the gilded drawing room with its crimson velvet walls, sumptuous enfilades, crystal girondoles, banked roses, and maidenhair fern that I was never sure that I had made the most of my opportunity of taking atmospheric period photographs; and the harassed but tactful stage manager always had to tap me on the arm and murmur, "Time, please."

Unless there is full confidence between sitter and photographer, the results may be far from satisfactory. Any preconceived knowledge the sitter may have about the best points of his or her appearance have a preliminary value, but problems are apt to arise when a sitter has too definite an idea as to how he or she should be photographed. During the sitting itself, the man behind the camera must always use his own judgment.

During one of my first visits to Hollywood I found Joan Crawford somewhat intractable. She arrived for her appointment wearing a halo toque of felt which she was loath to remove; with a dissatisfied pout she looked steadfastly, with hand on hip and shoulders raised, away from the camera so as to show the whites of her eyes. It was for me to take her in that pose, but I had seen too many pictures of Miss Crawford taken in this manner and I was not impressed. Slight compromises were made, but there was no real give and take between us; and only five plates had been exposed before we called off the sitting.

Mrs. Vernon Castle, who had been the object of my frenzied schoolboy admiration, came out of her retirement in Chicago to the house in which we then lived in Sussex Gardens to pose in a floating chiffon dress with the long slender waistline which she had made so personal. During her dancing career Mrs. Castle had always insisted on stage-managing her own photographs, and the results were certainly full of movement and fluid grace. But I found that to take pictures according to her formula was some-

Dorothy Hyson as Lady Windermere

Mrs. Vernon Castle

thing that gave me little scope for my customary arrangements. Still, I would try to be accommodating.

At her request a full-length looking glass was brought downstairs to stand beside my camera; a Panatrope gramophone played waltzes while she floated about the drawing room. "How's this?" Mrs. Castle would ask while she did her famous backward bend. But from where the camera was stationed there was nothing of my sitter to be seen. By the time I had focussed her in the centre of my picture, she was off again, carried around the room by the music, like a piece of thistledown. It was not until I had abruptly stopped the gramophone and removed the cheval glass from the room that I was able to photograph her in the only way I knew, though I must admit they had not the airy lightness of those I had secretly torn from the magazines belonging to the headmaster's wife when I was at my first boarding school.

Sir Max Beerbohm also had definite views and would allow himself to be photographed only against a black background. He insisted on having a chair and a table placed thus—and thus, and he would put up a hand to his face and hold onto a malacca cane; but at the possibility of a striped awning encroaching on the pictures he became rather anxious. When returning the proofs of his pictures he wrote:

They are all admirable likenesses of me. But I can't bear the striped curtain that appears in most of them, nor the wavering pallor of the other curtains. It is too ornamental for my years. Please let only the two with the unrelieved background be printed. I am sorry to be so fussy. But I did, on the telephone (before you went to America), say that I must have a quite plain setting. And when I came to the studio I thought the stripes at right angles to the black background would not come within the scope of the lens, and that the black background would be black every time; otherwise I would have uttered a frantic warning!

I am always surprised that in a photographic session there should be so few accidents. In photography, unlike the theatre, nothing is rehearsed. The studio is a hive of booby traps with wires to trip up a clumsy person and flimsy walls that he can easily knock over. Somebody might be electrocuted, or the heavy boom light above the sitter's head might one day come crashing down.

My photographic career has not been without its mishaps, the first of which occurred when the Edwardian beauty, Lily Langtry, was being photographed in the drawing room at Sussex Gardens. I had seen Mrs. Langtry in the South of France, and though she was by now an old woman, I had marvelled at the violet blue of her eyes and her still classic profile. Admittedly she had grown somewhat heavy; but with a certain ingenuity on my part, she could still be photographed in the likeness of the original "Jersey Lily." I draped her in black velvet, put a giant auratum lily at her bosom, and bade her proffer her famous profile. An enormous electric bulb had been placed at the back of her head in order to give her Greek chignon an aureole. Suddenly, for no reason that I know, the lamp went off with an enormous report. Mrs. Langtry ran around the room with her beautiful head ducked beneath her hands, shouting, "Am I on fire? Am I on fire?" The shock of the loud explosion on the elderly woman was horrible to see; but although no irreparable damage was done, she had to be revived with brandy.

One day early in my career the publicity expert of Madame Schiaparelli came to see me. Would I care to photograph Madame? Because Madame would like so much to give my sister a present of an evening dress. I did not know Madame Schiaparelli but admired enormously the dresses by which she was teaching the world her especial ideas of aesthetics.

On the day appointed for the sitting a publicity expert accompanied Madame Schiaparelli, and from her nervous manner she was obviously feeling the weight of her responsibility. Somehow everything went wrong: the paper backgrounds would not remain in place; the lights would not go on, although Manley, the butler, was on all fours under the grand piano checking electric switches. The local electrician was summoned. At last, when the lights blazed on in a flood of artificial sunshine, the silver-screen background crashed to the ground, bringing with it a gargantuan glass accumulator jar—fashionable at this time—which was filled with lilies. The drawing room was flooded, and the publicity expert and Madame looked on in acute embarrassment, while Manley, Miss Joseph, and I proceeded to do the necessary swabbing. Just as we thought we had the situation in hand, a new rivulet would course across the parquet floor straight towards Madame Schiaparelli's golden sandals. It is quite remarkable how much water a huge glass bowl can contain. I still do not know why, with so many electric wires lying in the puddles, some of us were not electrocuted. In spite of this disastrous first encounter, Madame Schiaparelli later so far forgave me that we went to Russia in the same party.

And then there was the distressing occasion when, one brilliant spring morning, I was photographing a delightful woman in her New York home. My sitter was posing against an enormous screen which had been painted for her by the late Boutet de Monvel. I was so intent on portraying my sitter to the best advantage, and the electrician was so busy loading the camera with more plates, that we neither of us noticed that a naked electric bulb, which I was in the habit of putting directly behind the sitter to clarify the

Lily Langtry. The last portrait of a great beauty.

outline of the figure, was by degrees being edged towards the screen. The sitter posed, hand on hip, this way, that way. Everything looked extremely elegant; the room was fragrant with primulas, daffodils, and narcissi. But suddenly the room became less fragrant; an appalling stench of scorching paint and canvas filled our nostrils. The back light had eaten a huge brown hole into the pristine whiteness of the Boutet de Monvel screen.

We considered the damage. It was severe, for the burning had taken place in the middle of the design; in fact, the valuable screen was utterly ruined. So great was my chagrin that it showed itself in a way that was unaccountable to my baffled sitter. Suddenly I started to laugh. I could not contain my amusement, and stood spluttering with convulsive jerks at the side of the camera. At last I thought I had recovered my equilibrium; but each time I tried to take another photograph I would tremble with asinine laughter as I held the trigger. I have seldom been more ashamed of myself, but the situation was beyond my control, and I had abruptly, and with great inner shame, to cancel the proceedings.

A somewhat similar catastrophe occurred when I was photographing a friend in my room at the Waldorf-Astoria and decided that her grey fox fur coat would be a more interesting background than the bogus panelling in my room. I hung the precious coat over a standard lamp and enthusiastically set to work. My sitter's ecstatic poses were suddenly interrupted by a foul smell of burning. We looked in horror to find the standard lamp bulb emerging through the scorched fur coat.

One Saturday morning, when posing like an angel of patience, a huge screen fell on Mrs. Harrison Williams, hitting her very forcefully on the crown of her beautiful head. The blow was so severe that Mrs. Williams had to be taken to see her doctor, and her week end was utterly ruined, for though she bore up at the time and behaved with her customary sweetness and charm, later in the day she suffered delayed shock and went to bed in tears.

On another occasion a heavy light crashed to the ground, missing Mrs. John Sutre's head by a few millimetres, but breaking her thumb on its transit, causing complications with X rays and doctors' diagnoses for many months to come.

After conducting so many thousands of photographic sittings during the last twenty years, I have developed a patter of which I am no doubt less conscious than my studio assistants. While I operate the camera I ceaselessly implore my sitters not to move, for few people understand that, however quickly one manipulates the shutter stops, the plates, and the focus knobs, the effect seen on the ground glass is changed the instant the sitters start to fidget and adjust hands or clothes. The success of a picture often depends on capturing those fleeting moments when draperies happen to fall in a particularly beautiful cascade or the hands are placed in a characteristic position. The more enthusiastic I become, the more often I reiterate, as to a baby: "Don't move! Don't move! Please don't move!" This plea has now become so automatic that an assistant recently told me that I had made it to a "still life."

Ina Claire, a friend for whom I have as much affection as admiration, is particularly erratic in her behaviour before the camera. Once after I had begged her continually, but in vain, to keep still, and again she immediately proceeded to ruin a pose by rearranging her skirt and hands, I lost control of my temper, stamped my feet, clapped my hands, and delivered a long and eloquent tirade of which I did not know that I was capable. Ina was so startled by my outburst that for the rest of the sitting she became as tractable as a good child; but I believe that ever since she has looked at me with a certain amount of suspicion.

However dull my sitters may seem on arrival, they can always be shown at their best advantage. They must always be given confidence, and to achieve the necessary relaxation and assurance I find myself speaking my thoughts aloud. If I manage my job in silence, I know instinctively the sitter becomes conscious of the unaccustomed quiet and may feel inclined to make conversation to me. This is disturbing and delays the final goal. Thus my assistants know by heart my reassuring patter. "That's wonderful! That's very interesting. This is 'very romantic,' 'mysterious' or 'compelling.'"

The only occasion on which any sitter has shown me open hostility was when, for a series of English composers, I was asked to photograph a little woman with something of a reputation in the artistic world. With starry eyes, a long rabbit face, and unruly hair, she appeared extremely *farouche* on arrival. I knew that this lady was the sister of a friend of mine and, hoping to break the ice, I mentioned the connection. Thereupon the composer went off in a diatribe against her sister and all her sister's friends and regarded me with uncompromising distaste. I cut short the scene by suggesting that she should face the camera; but no sooner had I begun to give my instructions than she at once resented the "bedside manner" I had automatically adopted. "Please don't treat me with such revolting politeness!" she cried. Would I kindly desist from such insincerity as to say she looked well? She knew she looked like a witch, that the whole thing was a mistake, and that she should never have come!

Somewhat abashed, I instructed her not to move. In so doing I must inadvertently have used my usual "camera-side" voice. "Oh God!" she

227

Mrs. Harrison Williams

shouted. "Stop that bloody cooing!" I conducted the rest of the sitting in a frustrated silence and felt it unfair that the results were quite unusually successful. The lady came out looking like the extraordinary character I am sure she is.

In dealing with the publication of my photographs in the general newspapers, I have weathered many storms. Photographs of the royal family inevitably produce complications; and when people not accustomed to appearing in the press wished their photographs to be published, there were also difficulties. In fact, there have been moments when I have sympathised with Dorothy Osborne's plea: "May I enjoy an early and a quiet grave, free from the trouble of this busy world, where All, with passion, pursue their own interests at their neighbours' charges; where Nobody is pleased but Somebody complains on't; and where it is impossible to be without giving and receiving injuries." Invariably the photograph which has been published is considered the only unsuccessful one from an entire sitting. The sitters, in almost every instance, wish to see a flattering and conventional picture of themselves, the editors of newspapers and magazines choose the most original or interesting print from the batch; hence mothers telephone in tears that the chances of their daughters' marriage have overnight become remote. I try my unsuccessful best to pacify the woman: "Oh no! Your daughter looks as if she has such character. Don't you see, she's a Goya!"

Chapter 12 *REFLECTIONS, TECHNIQUES, MODELS, AND BEAUTIES*

WHEN first I had the idea of writing this book I asked certain people to give their impressions of my photography. Many kind persons have replied at length.

I wrote to Dr. Agha, Condé Nast art director in the thirties, asking if he could care to contribute to my book. He replied, sending me many amusing anecdotes. Some of them I had forgotten; some I had not heard before—for instance, the editor who said that the picture would be taken against the usual Beaton background of soiled white satin. But what pleased me most about Dr. Agha's letter was the first paragraph: "I hope you will not be too modest and will show clearly that practically all of the devices, trends, and techniques that make today's photography (or at least fashion photography) what it is were originated or first used by you."

I also asked Jack, who first worked as my assistant in New York in 1935 and who today develops my negatives in the darkroom on Lexington Avenue, for his impressions of my photographic peculiarities, and he told me that I have always had a tendency to overexpose my negatives. I know this must be a result of my early battles against insufficient light. Jack tells me, too, that I am likely to "burn out" the sitter's hair by putting too strong a light on it; and this, too, I know is attributable to my experiences of twenty years ago when I worked with an inadequate camera and the pictures so often came out with a flatness of lighting. He also pointed out that I was the first fashion photographer to pose mannequins in ballet attitudes of mock surprise, ecstasy, or horror, and the first to place the model in "dancing mistress second position" with one foot pointed towards the camera—an attitude which, seen through the camera's eye, has the effect of elongating the body and is now to be observed in almost every fashion picture.

When I asked Truman Capote to give me his opinion, he said he considered I was first and foremost a recorder of fantasy. He added that through the years I have documented and illuminated the exact attitude of the moment.

When many years ago Bernard Shaw said that photography is like the cod which produces a million eggs in order that one may reach maturity, he was giving an accurate description of the small-camera photography of today. The current tendency is toward Leica shots of arrested movement—the more violent, the better. But although this method may produce results that could never be attained by careful planning in a studio, it is not a form of photography that demands an artist behind the camera. As much credit should be given to the art director who chooses, with discrimination, the one interesting freak shot out of a hundred snapshots as to the photographer who has taken what amounts to a "still" motion-picture strip.

When photography began, three or four exposures might be allotted for each sitting, but today an assignment with miniature cameras may result in five hundred exposures. When I took my first photographs my pocket money did not allow for a reckless expenditure of films. Each picture was a matter of serious consideration, and a large proportion of failures would have been disastrous. I would take perhaps four or six—at most eight—pictures at a time; and, as the exposures were always long and my sitter seldom remained motionless, my cod was often barren.

Today I use two cameras—a big one for the studios, a small Rolleiflex for my snapshots. With the big one, which gives results that are sharper and better for reproduction, I find I am somewhat limited as to pose and am apt to take studied, lifeless pictures and to photograph my sitters as if they were part of a frieze. These studied pictures are the amplification of all I have learned about photographic flattery, and the snapshot camera gives me more scope for plastic and character posing. At the beginning of my career, when I was less interested in my sitters as personalities than as lay figures in a fantasy, I coaxed them into uncomfortable attitudes against artificial backgrounds. In recent years they have been seen more often in their natural surroundings and, I trust, more or less characteristic attitudes; the background nowadays really is the background. . . .

For my studio work I have about half a dozen stock-in-trade décors. Whenever I am in doubt about how to photograph a certain subject I am apt to produce a blown-up photographic enlargement of Fragonard's "Swing" in the Wallace Collection, from which the young lady airily disporting herself in space has been obliterated. The foliage is so miraculously painted that I am always enchanted to discover how different the lighting effects appear on each new batch of photographic proofs. I have a background

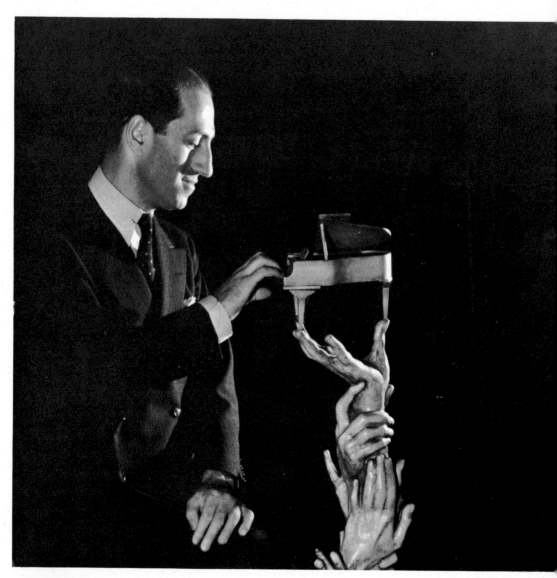

George Gershwin

of a Piranesi engraving, an architectural view of receding columns (the Queen once said, "I don't quite like the idea of being photographed in a tunnel"), a variety of details of trees taken from paintings by Breughel, Watteau, or from nature itself. Sometimes through a taxi window I catch sight in a shopwindow of a piece of tapestry, a chair, or brocade, which later is brought to the studio for one special occasion, but often I rely on any haphazard arrangement which occurs to me at the last minute.

I remember once seeing a remarkable object in a piano-shop window in New York—a plaster decoration of many hands, one above another, the uppermost holding aloft a miniature pianoforte. This I had planned to use for a photograph of George Gershwin. One afternoon I passed this shop in the company of George Huene, who was then photographing for the rival *Harper's Bazaar*. Suddenly he paused and gazed in the shopwindow. My heart missed a beat lest he should be inspired to use my treasure, and I was wondering whether I dared to claim priority, when he suddenly remarked, "I think something very interesting could be done in a photograph using a grand piano."

"Yes, George, I quite agree," I replied, "but do let's hurry along now or we'll be late."

There is the element of magic in exposing a plate and afterwards waiting to see the image that has been caught for permanence appear on the negative. After each sitting I leave the studio feeling that an exciting legacy is coming to me. As I have gained my experience I am able to work more and more speedily, with the result that today I err on the side of carelessness and lack of conscientiousness. It is seldom that I spend more than half an hour over a sitting. In that time one has to project one's own personality to the sitter; the technique is, in many ways, like that of a vaudeville artist who must almost immediately establish contact with the audience. It is no help to dawdle, whispering to one's assistants about the technical problems. If one shows no interest in the model, that lack of interest will appear in the result; one must give the sitter continual confidence and reassurance. Sometimes it is difficult to do this while manipulating the camera. Taking photographs requires great concentration; one has to be alert for every possible visual advantage that may come one's way; there are so many different details, all to be brought together in harmony when the shutter opens. It is the personal microscopic inspection of each sitter that has made the job so interesting to me.

Sometimes I have noticed that young women are apt to giggle nervously or react rather shyly when during the procedure of photography I have peered intently at them from behind the apparatus, made extremely personal observations about their appearance, or remarked upon the way they comported themselves. A sympathetic understanding between cameraman and his sitter is essential, for seldom does the photographer record anything interesting merely by opening the lens of his camera. If the sitter is putting up a resistance, the photographer must try to break down those reserves; and the cleverer the photographer is at this technique, the better his output is likely to be. The art of approaching a subject with a reassuring intimacy, yet without causing resentment, is often based on timing. If one feels by some remark one has exaggerated this intimacy or has treated the subject without sufficient deference, it is possible to withdraw at once, and indirectly suggest that those observations were merely made as part of the job in progress, that not for a moment was the intention to be personal, but one is, after all, merely a humble artisan doing the best.

Of recent years I have paid only the most cursory visits to the darkroom. Sometimes I regret that I do not spare more time in producing my own prints, for there is no doubt that the artist's personality comes through in the many decisions he makes during processing; and sometimes the achievements of technical accuracy destroys the human element. I respect and admire the efficiency of the technicians who can get the best possible results from my still sometimes erratic exposures, and I know that the straightforward technical part of the proceedings is in better hands than mine. I do not approve of trickery in the processing and consider that oil printing and solarisation are an admission that the negatives are not good enough to rely on their own merits. Goethe said, "In the end, of course, it is through the spirit that technique becomes alive."

The present-day swing away from Edward Steichen's and Edward Weston's technical perfection has resulted in all manner of tricks being employed in order to produce blurred images. I feel that one of our leading photographers is too violent when, in order to procure a dramatic picture, he kicks his camera-stand during an exposure. Though few of the young photographers may know it, the new out-of-focus pictures of mannequins with gaping goldfish mouths, caught in arrested movement, are all directly descended from Baron de Meyer; the only real difference being that, whereas De Meyer made his models proffer their stomachs, those of today have obviously been hit in the diaphragm.

Since my early attempts at photography, even when portraying my more fashionable and artificial-looking sitters, I have not relied upon the process of retouching in order to make them look their best. In fact, I have often envied the skill with which some commercial photographers are able to flatter their clients solely by this means. I have never known how to "paint in" a new face in place of the old, and if my sitter does not look passable in the untouched proof, there is small chance of her becoming a beauty merely by knifing and pencilling on the negative. If I have been able to take flattering likenesses of my feminine sitters, it is because they have been caught from the most advantageous angle, in the light most becoming to their particular mould of feature, and wearing their most agreeable expression; for even the ugliest woman has her good points.

An enormous improvement upon the image registered by the camera lens can be brought about on the negative by "cleaning-up," "slenderising," obliterating unwelcome veins and shadows, and by lightening the hair. In fact, most women come to accept their likeness after beautification as the true one, and they are horrified to see themselves as they appear to the camera's relentless eye before the beautifier's treatment. Today the editors of certain periodicals encourage their staff photographers to become "realists" and to aim, it seems, at catching their prey at its most characteristic, or perhaps least fortunate, moment. The results are not so entertaining to the sitters as to the public.

I enjoy the ritual of selecting the best proofs of each sitting and then "marking" them for embellishment. To make these directives to the retoucher, generally done in thick ink strokes, gives one an enormous satisfaction; for, as one slices down the outline of a protruding stomach and brings about miraculous changes to an unfortunate contour, one feels like a magician. With a bold stroke one lops off pounds of flesh from one woman, twenty years from another. The photographer soon comes to think of his instructions on the rough proofs as a *fait accompli,* but if these corrected prints should by some mischance be seen by others, the effect must be startling. The sitter, trying to look dignified, has arrows pointing to the back of her neck indicating the dotted line to which she must be pared down—similar lines mark the reshaping of her stomach and her behind; and a further series show the unwelcome shadows on her upper lip, which must be smoothed and cleaned, and the shadows at her nostrils, giving the effect of an unpleasant smirk, which the retoucher must obliterate.

On one occasion a most regrettable mistake was made. An acquaintance of mine, about to be married, wished me to photograph his bride-to-be as a wedding present, and the pictures were duly taken. His affianced could not by any standards be considered a beauty, and I looked at the rough proofs in despair. Her pictures could never be beautiful, but the retoucher and I would certainly try to give her every aid. I wielded the pen on the rough proofs with an outrageous abandon. For the retoucher's guide I sliced the hips in half, cut the neck almost in two, remodelled the arms, flattened the behind, raised the bosom, and darkened all the face shadows to indicate where they must be retouched. I felt the retoucher would hardly be able to believe I wished such drastic alterations, so onto the prints I added written directions:

Dear Miss Roberts, please do your best—or your damnedest. We've *got* to make this wretched woman look passable. She's going to be married next week, and we must try to help her make a success of it, so, *please,* cut her down by half, tighten her girth, put some life into her hair, and give her the semblance of a neck. God gave her no eyes, but see what you can do. Paint in lashes, cut off her dark moustachios, make her fingers look long and delicate, and not like the little trotters they are!

At this time my secretary went on her summer holidays; an assistant—willing, but not experienced—took her place. The bridegroom rang up. When shall he see the bride's pictures? Remember, the wedding is fixed for the day after tomorrow. Would we try to get them finished by tomorrow evening? This meant Miss Roberts's working her fingers to the bone, possibly till the early hours. But at the eleventh hour the pictures came back from Miss Roberts, who proved to have surpassed herself. When you compared the horrifying rough proofs, the finished pictures were enchanting. A monster had been turned into a beauty. Splendid. No time to lose. I handed them to my temporary secretary. "Will you have them taken around by special messenger right away?"

Unfortunately my temporary secretary sent round to the bridegroom-to-be not only the finished pictures but also the rough proofs marked with my retouching directives, so that he could fully appreciate Miss Roberts's handiwork when comparing the two sets of proofs. The wedding took place the following day, but I doubt if it was wholly my fault that after a few months the marriage came to an acrimonious end.

The retouching of negatives is usually a long job. My sitters seldom realize how much careful miniature work must go into the beautifying process before they can see the proofs. Often I find they want their photographs taken for a specific date and have not allowed enough time, so that telegrams have to be sent backwards and forwards concerning the delivery of the pictures. Not all are so pernickety as the lady whose letter follows. Nevertheless, it typifies the reactions of a certain type of sitter.

Dear Miss ——, I'm so sorry I'm afraid I could never quite catch your name each time we have spoken on the telephone—so stupid of me! Thank you for your telegram in answer to mine. I did not wire you back because I have so many suggestions to make about the retouching. Unfortunately, my husband and mother, or any of my friends, are not too pleased with the photographs. They all say they don't do me justice, and they don't think they are a credit to Mr. Beaton's reputation. In fact, they say this does not look like his usual work which is so divinely glamorous etc. etc. I know I looked a perfect fright that day, and my friends begged me to cancel the sitting at the last moment, saying I looked too terrible, but I hated to do this as the arrangements with Mr. Beaton had taken so long to make, and I had put Mr. Beaton off so many times before, and I did want to be taken with my boys before they grow up any taller (already they make me look so aged!) and in my Balenciaga and Hartnell gowns while they were still fresh and of this season. You see, my trouble is that I get too tired, and when I'm tired I go to pieces and I look like the original Frankenstein. I must admit I had been out too late during the previous two months, and had seldom got to bed before four o'clock and I had lost twelve pounds and my husband said I looked like a scarecrow. I thought Mr. Beaton would be able to rectify this, but he has made me look as if I'd been putting on weight! I am only a size ten and a half with a thirty-five bust, but Mr. Beaton has greatly enlarged my figure and I look gigantic. What is worse is Mr. Beaton has played havoc with my nose and mouth. He has lengthened the upper lip making the space between the nose and the lip enormous. The ones in the tiara are the only ones that are like me. In all the others I have got what my mother calls my "poultice face"—all very swollen and peculiar. I don't want to order any just now because I'm almost dead with the rush of Christmas shopping, but if ever I survive these hectic weeks I will then go carefully into the matter again thoroughly, but in the meantime I am sending back some of the proofs for further retouching so that I can see if, when all these alterations are done, I like the pictures, or would prefer to sit again to Mr. Beaton in my spring season's clothes. In any case, when I ask to see these pictures again, why don't you include all the proofs? You sent me only twenty-four finished pictures and I'm certain Mr. Beaton must have taken at least fifty-seven or fifty-eight. I asked my maid to count during the sitting, and she said he'd taken five times as many as any of the other London photographers, and believe me, we've been to them all, so why doesn't he let me see the lot? It may be that I'd like some that had caught some fleeting expression that is essentially "me" although it might not appeal to Mr. Beaton.

These are the main corrections I would advise: First of all the hair. I don't know how he could have done it, but in all these pictures Mr. Beaton has made me look practically bald. Don't you see what a thin hairline he has given me? You can see my scalp shining through in some where the light is so much too strong. If Mr. Beaton hadn't shown obvious impatience at my taking so long to get prepared in the dressing room, and had allowed me to go back there once I had come out, then I could have fixed these curls to give a softer appearance. I have already admitted I had a very swollen face that day, especially about the eyes; I must have looked like an old suet pudding! My husband said he had not seen me with such a terrible face for years, and he was horrified. He said, what had I been up to! Mr. Beaton will remember that he refused to allow me to put on any more make-up. He said I had been drastic enough. Do you think that it would now help if the heavy lids you have already softened were removed entirely, and the eyes made to look as if they were wide open? Please ask Mr. Beaton to use his retouching magic to turn a truly sick-looking person into the semblance of a human being. God knows I'm not a beauty, but we all like to look our best, and Mr. Beaton has done such wonders with others in the past.

I am not interested in any of the photographs of my sons. They do not come out at all well, but I might like to have one of the groups if you could fix up their faces a bit too. They have such terrible circles under their eyes. These have only appeared quite recently—since they went to Eton in fact. I do hope something can be done about it as they were both such pretty boys until only a short while ago. However, I don't suppose it's all that important for men to be good-looking, is it? Do see that Mr. Beaton really concentrates on me, and takes his time about it. Thanks! And a Happy Christmas!

Since I became a professional photographer I have only rarely photographed strangers who telephone for an appointment. I learned quickly enough that these sittings are always accompanied by the maximum of trouble. Having asked, at great length, my secretary's advice and my own about what she should wear, then decided to wear something quite different, changed the date of the appointment several times, and eventually arrived an hour late, the unknown sitter finally exhibits herself as an overdressed, over-fed, pampered woman who, weeks later, announces that she is disappointed with the results of the sitting and decides that she would like to have the pictures retaken, is retaken in a different set of dresses, and at last comes to the conclusion that she prefers the original batch. In these circumstances it is scarcely surprising that, on the whole, I would rather work for a magazine, photographing ladies who are accustomed to being photographed and who know more or less what the results will be.

I have often found that the most beautiful women, those whom one would expect to be most critical of their pictures, are the most readily pleased and most grateful with the work I have done of them; even when, secretly, I have not considered that they have been done by worthily. I have seen enough of the certain wealthy middle-class woman to realise how strong are her illusions about the way she looks; and my heart goes out to those who are at her mercy in dress and hat shops.

I have also noted with pain how many people, considered extremely "well off," are wretchedly bad bill payers. They will agree to the price of a sitting, seem extremely pleased with the results, and then when the bill is sent ignore it completely. When one's friends behave in this manner, it is too disheartening to send in repeated requests over the years; and many a time, after considerable outlay, I have had to forgo any thought of recompense.

Often I am approached by worthy people who beg me, for some special purpose, to take photographs that they know they are unable to afford. In many instances I am delighted to be of help, for I feel my contribution is greater than if *I* were to make a financial gift. Many of my most interesting pictures have been taken in the knowledge that I could expect no profit; and when any gratitude is shown for my efforts I feel fully recompensed. Sometimes I have been delighted when a sitter, unable to pay my bill, sends a token present. I have received some very peculiar pots and vases, tortoise-shell fans, mother-of-pearl ribbon boxes, cigars, preserved fruit, and extremely expensive cartons of flowers instead of a cheque. Once the front-door bell rang, and Lady Oxford's chauffeur handed in an enormous fruit dish of Venetian glass with the enchanting note from which I am sure she would not, were she alive, mind my quoting:

4.30 a.m. 21st July '31
This hour is *not* the time I left the ball, as I was in bed by 12:30; now I often wake at these hours. My dear, I think you not only a very great artist, but one of the kindest men I ever knew, and I thank you for photographing me. Do you imagine that I am not *grateful* to you, because I am. If I had a farthing in the world (or in my bank) I w'd pay you highly for your proficiency. But, alas! I am up to my eyes in debt. I suppose I am frivolous, as I accept all grand invitations, court banquets, etc., wh all cost me money wh I can't afford. I am unluckily dog-poor, and I daresay *you* are also. All I can say in my defence is that I am very grateful to all who help me, and this *you* do. You are the only man who can make a *plain* woman interesting. I think the full face looking down with the pale earrings a work of genius. I am sending you a dish to put grapes or oranges or any fruit you like upon, to show you, though I am poor, and ought to retire from London life, I am grateful.

It is the spadework involved in arranging each sitting that mitigates against the pleasures of photography. I have never been able to organise my life so that a secretary takes entire control over all the technical side of my photographic work, nor would this be beneficial to the results. A personal touch must be given to the pictures, and this has to be done by me alone. Unless I mark for retouching each print myself, some defect will be missed or some detail will not be to my liking. Each finished print may need a certain amount of pencilling and checking without which I know my sitter will rightly be dissatisfied.

There are so many processes through which the photographs must pass before being delivered to the sitter or to the press. It involves a constant messenger service, prints coming backwards and forwards in their various stages of completion. Suddenly, while having a bath, I will remember that a certain print has not been seen through its total journey. After careful investigation it transpires that I was out at the moment a messenger called and, as the picture was needed for reproduction by the blockmaker by a certain time, they would not wait. It is now too late to save the situation, and because I was not there to check, the picture about to be reproduced in the magazine is the very one the sitter has forbidden for publication, and quite rightly, for she is not looking her best and the required effect of formality is ruined by the electrician, who can be clearly seen adjusting a plug underneath the lady's chaise longue.

Although each sitting may take but a short time, the countless details, endless telephone calls, arrangements, and rearrangements usurp many hours in the day of a successful photographer. When at last the long labyrinth of arrangements concerning each sitting has been traversed, one feels another of life's milestones has gone by.

I am fortunate in that I can, to some extent, choose my own subjects; and many of them are interesting personalities who react to the operation in their individual, and somewhat surprising, manner. Lady Astor had intended for many years to sit for me, but she always "cried off" at the last moment. She would excuse herself by saying, "I am not as I was when Sargent painted me, and I am not yet old enough to be photographed as Whistler's Mother, and the 'in-between' is horrid." One day, however, I prevailed upon her to delay no longer. She came to the studio with her most magnificent jewels; but, just as I felt we were getting into our photographic stride, Lady Astor began to consider I was spending much too much time on her.

"Surely that's enough! To take so many pictures is madness!"

But my enthusiasm for this remarkable woman continued as she kept up a continuous stream of amusing comments and did brilliant imitations of Americans, Welshmen, and Scots, while I continued to click the lens.

At last she exploded, "But it's not healthy for you to spend so much time lookin' at an old woman's face!"

But I continued to watch her like a hawk.

At length she said, "Well, if *you're* not mad, it's *me* that's goin' mad." And she asked me, "Would you like to photograph the woman who went mad while being photographed by Cecil Beaton?"

Lady Astor is able to screw her features into a ball; no school child knows more horrible facial tricks. She now pulled every inconceivable face. The effects were hardly human. As she continued to make these grimaces, the assistants from the darkrooms upstairs crept down the circular iron staircases to look on in awed amazement and admiration at this fantastic display, some of which has been recorded for private perusal only.

When photographing Lady Bath and her family at Longleat, which had been recently opened to the public, the great house resounded to the echoes of lady guides in various rooms saying, "This is the third Marquis," "Do look at this cut Genoese velvet," "Do you see this old piece of armour?" I had chosen, perhaps unwisely, for my photographic session the long tapestried gallery. Here Lady Bath, her daughter and niece, all wearing the billowing flounces of their latest ball dresses, were posing in romantic attitudes, when suddenly the doors were flung open and the public was thrown among us. Great confusion ensued. The guides strove to persuade their charges to look at the fine screens, the tapestry, the Renaissance ceilings; but all eyes were on the strange domestic scene confronting them. Amid shy giggles we heard exclamations of "Oh! They're wearing the old family clothes." "Oh! Isn't it a *shame!*" "Poor Lady Bath! It isn't fair on her! I know times have changed, but we really oughtn't to be here! The poor wretches can't even be photographed in peace!"

Today, when photographers even stand in the streets snapping passers-by in the hope of finding an occasional "client," sitters are seldom overcome by Victorian shyness; only now and then do any of my sitters display camera nerves. Once, for example, I had the greatest difficulty in stopping my sitter from whistling. Another time a friend of mine came to be photographed wearing a new dress, with her hair beautifully coiffed. Her appearance was evidently the result of many hours of hard work, but when she stepped before the camera she swayed from side to side in paroxysms of giggles. I discovered that, to fortify herself against the ordeal, she had taken "a short one," then another, until she was quite drunk. I was very angry and felt there was nothing to giggle about.

Rarely do I ask my sitters to smile. If they can do so naturally, I am delighted, for I feel that the fashion for sullen beauties glowering at the world has gone on too long, but an invitation to smile has sometimes had results more painful to me than to my victim; the smile has developed into a nervous twitch, or the lower part of the jaw quivered like a jelly. There are moments when a smile goes dry over the sitter's teeth and the process of bringing the lips back to their former position is dreadful to behold.

Once in New York I asked an extremely sullen sophisticate, whose customary expression was a frown, if she could smile for the camera. She glowered at me.

"Why, sure, if you just tell me at the time of clicking, but I can't hold it for long."

My nephew, John Smiley

My niece, Rosamond Hambro

I gave the word "Go." I had expected a slow smile to illuminate the sullen features. But no! The frowning beauty suddenly exposed her teeth in the most diabolical grimace. This was switched off almost as instantaneously and surprisingly as it had appeared. My assistants and I were dumfounded, and I was not quick enough to open the shutter. I decided we must try again. The beauty, meanwhile, was once more contentedly glowering over a cigarette.

"Would you please give another of your spontaneous smiles?"

She did. It was an unbelievable performance. So appalling was the effect, so far removed from a smile, and so great the conceit of this lady at her histrionic accomplishment, that it was difficult for the witnesses not to show their amusement. This was a rare treat which we must not cut short. My assistants and I had an enjoyable time exposing plate after plate for the pleasure of studying the effect of this most remarkable demonstration. With assumed sincerity I complimented the sitter on her ability to give the photographer everything he could hope for; and I really believe she thought she had mastered the art of spontaneity.

Recently, rather than ask women of the world to come to the studio to be photographed for the magazines, it has been more fashionable to take them in their own houses or apartments. These excursions into the intimacy of strangers' houses has a rather sinister fascination for me. Sometimes before my arrival the owner of the house has heard of my name and treats me as a guest; but often I find I am invading the privacy of some unknown person, where I am treated like a tradesman, with civility but distant arrogance. This role gives me a new perspective on life, and for a short time I enjoy adopting an obsequious manner, making no conversational efforts, and eyeing everything around me from a dispassionately critical point of view. In a friend's house one's opportunities of observation are necessarily limited; but the photographer-tradesman can, without offence, take an inventory of the contents and announce that it includes nothing that suits his personal taste.

I have often been astonished to see in what uncomfortable and tasteless surroundings many of the so-called privileged classes live. In New York, apartments are badly proportioned, and there is seldom an object or piece of furniture of the slightest merit or value. In London, rooms are shabby, needing a coat of paint and, in winter, inadequately heated. As for Paris—it is amazing to discover that the French princesses, duchesses, comtesses, and baronesses who form the pivot of French society, even when they belong to the wealthiest families in France, live in conditions of drab tastelessness. Spending money where it can be seen is perhaps a French characteristic. These ladies may have wonderful jewels, and occasionally they buy one extremely "important" dress; but their apartments produce no effect of being "lived in." Cheap modernistic furniture is dumped about without any reference to family relics; there are seldom any flowers in the vases, and no servants to answer bells. The dining room of the wife of one of France's greatest sugar magnates fascinated me. The walls were hung with Cecil Aldin reproductions of hunting scenes in rough oak frames alongside Fougita engravings in mirror and silver frames. In the centre of the dining table was a large modernistic travelling clock, while, propped against the wainscot, were such objects as an ironing board, a bicycle, and a pair of riding boots.

On one occasion I went to take photographs in a room decorated by one of the most advanced and exaggeratedly fantastic of modern interior decorators. As we drove towards the address given us we were surprised to find ourselves in one of the more squalid suburbs of Paris, and as we approached a pepper-coloured brick house in a row of other similarly hideous buildings we felt we must be mistaken. We pulled a rusty doorbell. Was it possible that the General So-and-so, owner of this latest triumph of interior decoration, lived here? Yes, the servant reassured us, it was perfectly true.

We mounted steps to a vestibule where some garden chairs were placed among perambulators and umbrella and croquet-mallet stands; a glimpse of a stuffy, rather badly smelling library with maps on the wall, a huge Victorian desk on which were piled many boxes of cigars. Down a dull corridor we went, with engravings of dogs on the walls, past a dining room like a dentist's waiting room. Then suddenly the guardian opened the drawing-room door. Before us was the latest fantasy of perverse decoration. Furniture made of majolica, of brass, with railway-coach chairs, curtains, and walls covered with a violent flowered chintz of ferns, heather, and violets, with pinnacle vases filled with the most extraordinary conglomeration of 1900 objects.

It was a room of the purest fantasy. How could one reconcile this room to the rest of the house? Had the general given the job of decorating his drawing room, out of kindness, to his nephew? What did he think when first he saw the transformation? What would his fellow generals think when they came in for a military chat? These incursions into other people's houses are fraught with drama and mystery; and for me the bathrooms of strangers have always had an especially morbid fascination.

There is, perhaps, a no more transient career than that of a successful fashion model. Even a Hollywood film star's life of fame lasts long in comparison. The highest-paid model in New York can hope for a successful span of five years during which she will be photographed every hour of the working week, and her face and figure will be seen everywhere. Then suddenly the proofs of this lady's pictures show unwelcome shadows at the neck, or her arms assume an unwelcome angularity, and the word goes round that she is "finished." What happens to her eventually, we do not discover.

Of the many hundreds of professional models I have photographed, I remember only a handful as at all outstanding. For example, Marianne Moorehouse, who, with her long coltish limbs, gazelle-like eyes, and sleek straight hair, was Steichen's greatest model of the twenties and gave distinction to every dress she wore. Helen Bennett, before the war, was fought over by all the photographers. She had an early Egyptian catlike beauty, with the flat curls of a Greek statue; her body was exotically attenuated and her poses those of insolent pride. After the war Andrea Johnson conveyed an extraordinary quality of feminine delicacy and sensitivity. Then came Jean Patchett, young, tall, and healthy, like a pale wicked cherub, with biscuit-coloured hair and skin and an entirely new set of attitudes; diaphragm gathered in, the top part of the body thrown forwards, a trailing foot—perhaps a reminiscence of Mrs. Vernon Castle—keeping the necessary balance. Currently Miss Patchett is the most-sought-after of all models, and she makes any fashion photographer's task easy.

But for what she can bring to a photographic sitting I consider Dorian Leigh by far the most intelligent, flexible, and interpretative of today's models. According to the dress or hat she must wear, she plays a different role; each sitting has a little acting in it, and Miss Leigh is an instinctive actress. If you saw her walking down Lexington Avenue you would not be particularly impressed by her appearance and would certainly never believe it possible that she is the highest-paid model in the world today. But as soon as she steps in front of a camera she assumes beauty in a hundred different forms. Her poses are seldom the same; she somehow senses what it is the photographer is inadequately trying to get from her, and she conveys a remarkable variety of moods. She can assume any age between twelve and fifty, and she can give an atmosphere of rarity to any garment. In the classical sense she is no beauty, but her delicate features can suggest the sweetness of an eighteenth-century pastel, the allure of a Sargent portrait, or the poignancy of some unfortunate woman who sat for Modigliani. Apart from these histrionic performances, she is intelligent and photogenic enough to play the part of the ordinary pretty model, whose appeal must reach to the furthest limits of the great American public.

The loveliest women of each period are seen at their best against a luxurious setting, or at any rate in a becoming frame. These postwar years have provided no framework for their professional beauties, and no longer are they given the attention that was lavished on Georgina, Lady Dudley, Lina Cavalieri, Liane de Pougy, Lily Langtry, or their contemporaries. Mere

Greta Garbo

classical beauty is not considered enough; our present-day idols must be intelligent as well as beautiful.

The Marquise de la Falaise is perhaps exceptional in that, besides being handsome in a classical sense, she suits the requirements of post-World War II fashions. Her limbs are so exaggeratedly elongated, her nose so small, her eyes so enormous, that she looks like a fashion drawing come to life. Moreover, she has developed the talent and courage to appear at her most striking while at the same time running the risk of looking merely freakish, her theory being that she looks her best in hard ugly clothes rather than in the traditional draperies of a classic beauty. The effect that she creates with her shingled Napoleonic hair, her long body tightly encased in tentlike stripes, and, from her ears, two hanging chandeliers, is spectacular.

Strangely enough, it is in Paris that this English lady, the daughter of the portrait painter, Sir Oswald Birley, is seen at her best. Very few beauties transplant well. I have seen beautiful English roses take the trip across the Channel to arrive looking jaded and tired; they have not recovered their freshness until they have returned to their native soil. The trip across the Atlantic is equally hard on even the most hardy specimens. American women seldom look their best in Paris, and Parisians are never seen at their greatest advantage in the United States. It is not so much a question of clothes as, perhaps, of line and proportion. In the brilliant light of New York, only the neatest and most immaculate New York woman can survive scrutiny unscathed.

Of all the women I have ever photographed, I would name, as the most consistently lovely, Lily Elsie, Lady Diana Cooper, Paula Gellibrand (later to become the Marchesa Casa Maury), the Duchess of Kent, and Greta Garbo.

Of all the women I have ever seen, Miss Garbo is by far the most beautiful. After our first encounter in Hollywood, many years passed before I met her again; but the passage of time had only improved her lunar beauty, given her features a more chiselled sensitivity and her expression a more touching nobility. We renewed our friendship, but I knew so well of her dislike of being photographed that, since she was not at this time appearing in moving pictures, I had no excuse to ask her to sit for me. I was quite resigned never to include her among my sitters, when one day she started to ask me a question which I noticed she could not bring herself to complete.

"I wonder if . . ." she would say, and then break off in a state of indecision. She told me that she was about to take her first trip abroad since the war, and again she started, "I wonder . . . If you weren't such a grand and elegant photographer . . ."

At once I knew what she wanted to ask me.

"Then you'd ask me to take a passport photograph for you?"

"How did you know?"

I realised it was impossible for Greta Garbo to visit an ordinary passport photographer without the results being advertised far and wide, so it was as a passport photographer that I took photographs of the face of this century, thereby achieving my greatest ambition and crowning my photographic career.

Chapter 13 SUMMING UP

AFTER the war I was expelled from my enchanted house among the Wiltshire downs. I had made many improvements there, and I was filled with chagrin when my landlord refused to renew my lease. For two years I searched, in vain, for some shell which I could make into a sympathetic retreat. I had begun to despair of ever finding any house I could like half so well as Ashcombe, when I received a telegram saying that a small Charles II house with a beautiful brick-and-stone façade and a high wall of topiary work, which I had long since admired as I drove through the neighbouring village of Broadchalke, was about to come on the market. Happily I was able to buy the house. From the moment I arrived at Redditch House I started a new photographic period. I found myself enthusiastically recording the changes that took place from week to week in the gardens and the surrounding woods, as early spring passed into summer, and the sweetness of high summer changed to the gradual sadness of the autumn months.

On several occasions the gardens were populated with fashion models from London and New York who posed in the most luxurious dresses in these idyllic and bucolic settings. But many times my camera was turned towards more simple subjects; I find that my most recent photographs are of the Maréchal Niel roses and clematis climbing on a wall, of a basket with gardening gloves, a trowel, and some strands of bass, or of trees, plants, and children. To try to document the fleeting moods of childhood has given me enormous pleasure: the nuances of expression are so much more varied than when an adult mask is worn. Children's faces have no secrets and their eyes are unguarded in their reactions to atmosphere and scene, becoming in turn tragi-serious or fecklessly gay. Recently, when I found myself taking photographs of my nieces in the cornfield beyond the paddock, I saw they were almost startlingly reminiscent of pictures I had taken of my sisters in the same setting at the beginning of my career.

In the library at Redditch House, a room I particularly love, I have collected in large red leather albums all my photographs which have appeared since first I started taking pictures. By now there are some forty of these albums, and the number of pictures among these hundreds of pages is so prodigious that I feel it is time I stopped adding to their number. They reveal so many evanescent moods and modes, so many forgotten people—and the survivors have already undergone such startling changes—that the impression they create is that of a photographic mausoleum.

Examining these pictures after a long interval, I was struck by the feeling of restlessness that my more frivolous work creates. I cannot understand why I was so seldom able to take a picture of any "society lady" without a great quantity of ornament in the composition. I seem rarely to have resisted the temptation of inserting in some corner the inevitable mass of ectoplasmic blossoms, a table draped with velvet or tinsel, a fluted column, Grinling-Gibbonesque pedestals, Corinthian capitals, paper roses or Mexican tinsel flowers, peacocks' feathers, ermine tails, sequins, polka dots, Christmas paper balloons, or whitened branches. Although they have proved less popular, I feel that my best work is among the straightforward portraits of personalities whose strength of appearance gave me solid material to work upon, of children whose diminutive faces express so much of the wonder and pathos of the world around them, and photographs taken during the war against the background of a battlefield.

It is difficult for any artist to analyse his own work; I cannot quite explain what I wish to achieve each time I take a photograph, for my aims and intentions may vary with each different subject. Although I agree with Man Ray that "photography is not art," I know that the process of taking photographs can be compared in certain ways to that of other art forms. One feels suddenly inspired to improvise, to elaborate, or to change one's tune. One becomes an operator sensitive to all sorts of mysterious vibrations. The photographer, dealing with human beings, is perhaps nearer to a film director than to the painter working quietly in his studio. Generalisations are often worthless; however, I think, quite by chance I hit upon a certain truth when, last summer, my gardens in the country were visited by a great number of enthusiastic amateurs from several camera clubs in the West of England. I was asked by their chairman if I could give any hints, rules, or advice on how the club members could take more successful photographs. I looked at the formidably complicated equipment they had with them; obviously they knew a great deal about metres, various coloured filters, and special lenses; I could be of no technical help to them, so I advised them to "break every photographic rule." Admittedly this advice is for those who know the rules so well that when breaking them they can gauge the effects they are about to create; but the most interesting experiments are nearly always those which contradict the "accepted" laws of picture making.

Although I am an admirer of the good clear photograph and, upon occasion, try to achieve an effect with the most straightforward means, I would never have made a reputation for myself as a manipulator of the camera if I had not used it for experiments and done things in my own way; a technical "failure" which shows some attempt at aesthetic expression is of infinitely more value than an uninspired "success." Although a number of my attempts at breaking away from the conventional have failed, those that succeeded have stimulated the imagination and remained in the mind.

In America photography has become a serious business medium. I would like to see English photography given more encouragement; for only in the New World do business executives fully appreciate the advantages of really good photography, and are willing to pay prices that tempt a photographer of talent or ambition. Hence the fact that the best photographers are working in America. Enormous prices are paid by advertisers for pictures that they know can be relied upon to pay dividends yet have little importance in the world of creative photography. Financially, the most successful photographers in business today are unoriginal technicians who have commercialised the talents of the real creative artists.

Although I am occasionally appalled at the amount of energy I still have to put into each photography session, there is always something dramatic about the job of permanently recording the features of a human being. It is the theater brought to everyday life; the ordinary routine of existence is broken, and the tension is heightened. It is this element which renews one's passion in photography with every interesting sitting and makes bearable even the dullest commercial assignment. However humdrum a subject may have seemed in advance, and however tired I have felt beforehand, once I am on the job, with its own difficulties to overcome, I am absorbed by it and find myself possessed of renewed strength.

I suppose most people have a secret ambition to be something other than they are. The critic wishes to be a playwright, the business executive a poet. In my own mind I have never decided that I am solely a photographer. In order not to feel tied to this branch of my work, I have never taken on the responsibility of a studio with a staff to keep me up to schedule. Perhaps this was an unconscious effort not to confine my capabilities. In effect I believe this has helped me to maintain a freer approach to the camera. Since the war

I have devoted more time and energy to my theatrical work, and at the moment I feel it is in this direction that my greatest interest lies. Not that I believe I have explored all the photographic horizons open to me, for every year they become wider and there is no limit to the range of experiment. So many elements go into the making of a remarkable photographer. His work reveals as much of his personality and character as it does of his sitter's. I know that to take good photographs one must continually keep one's hand in, but in future I would like photography to play a less important role in my professional existence. I trust I shall never altogether abandon photography: it has brought me much happiness and I have no regrets that it is as a photographer I have spent so many years; all branches of my work have a great affinity. At one period of my life when I was acting on Broadway in *Lady Wildermere's Fan,* as the run of the play progressed and I gained more flexibility and confidence in my part, I knew that I had learned a great deal about acting in the photographic studio, where timing, spontaneity, and projection of personality are equally important as on the stage. The personal element shapes a photographer's career just as it does an actor's, a politician's, or a lawyer's. Once I had won the sympathy and gained the confidence of a number of my sitters, and proved myself a trustworthy artist, I could proceed to turn my medium to some genuinely aesthetic purpose.

Today when young people write asking me to advise them on the benefits of a photographic career, I have to warn them of some of the disadvantages. A painter or draughtsman learns more with every sketch he makes, and his pictures usually increase in quality and in value. But the advance a photographer makes every time he takes a picture is infinitesimal; and the commercial value of a photograph is extremely short-lived. For old photographs the market is almost non-existent, so that the moment the photographer fails to keep up to date he ceases to be able to earn a living. For the photographer, unlike the writer, there can be no period of relaxation while he lives on royalties. I have made a considerable amount of money, though not as much as I am said to have made or should actually have made. Photography is an expensive business; overhead costs soar. Unless you are a most successful photographer, you can expect small compensation for dogged hard work and frequent disappointments.

If a photographer is outstandingly successful, he suffers from the danger of his work becoming repetitious; his popularity often depends on his knack of giving a recognisable stamp to every sitting. The successful photographer is the man who, in addition to the talents of an artist, possesses those of a journalist. For there is no profit in taking photographs seen once a year by the limited number of people visiting a photographic exhibition; his pictures must "make news," and nearly always the news is his subject rather than the photographer's art. I attribute the position I hold as a photographer not so much to opportunity, luck, adaptability or hard work, or even to the qualities of my photographs themselves, as to the fact that I am intensely interested in a large variety of people whose tastes are often far removed from my own. Many times during the war I noticed that other photographers, who could have done technically better work, failed to get certain commissions which were entrusted to me, because they showed not enough curiosity in their fellow human beings.

You may ask why it is not possible to combine a photographic career with other work. But there are many difficulties. The nervous excitement of a sitting creates a feeling of tension that cannot immediately be discarded for a more sober mood. No matter how short a time a sitting may have taken, I come away from the studio after that sitting with very much less energy than when I arrived, and on that day am in no mood to embark upon the rigorous task of being a painter, writer, or dramatist. When taking photographs, only certain portions of the brain are called into action; but at the end of a day, physically exhausted through using my powers of instinctive observation, because other powers have remained unused, I am apt to feel dissatisfied.

Although we are often told that success spoils, I know that I myself should have been spoiled by failure. Moreover, success in photography has helped me to study many aspects of life that I might not have otherwise seen, and has enabled me to observe at close quarters a vast variety of men and women. I have few regrets, for photography has provided a fascinating career, involving me in many exciting, even historical, events. I have even learned a little about human nature.

Recently I came across Henry Green, the writer and an old friend, who, on seeing me at the same photographic routine, exclaimed sympathetically, "My God! You must be bored by the racket by now!" I was amused: photography is no more a racket than any other art form, and certainly it is to me less boring than going each day to an office in order to earn one's living. But my friend's outburst fired me to take stock of myself. I realised that nowadays, although I am never bored while I am on the job, nevertheless I undertake to do too much photographic work that does not give me an opportunity to express myself fully. Yet each time I come across a human being of real worth and integrity I am given a new incentive to creativity, just as each time I arrive in some new country I see my unaccustomed surroundings with an eye undimmed by familiarity, and something in the change of atmosphere inspires me to take photographs and always gives them a fillip of freshness and new feeling.

Throughout my photographic career I have always felt that in five years' time I should no longer be a photographer. At this moment I still feel that in five years' time I shall have given up photography except on very rare occasions. But more than twenty years have now elapsed since I first started clicking the shutter of my camera as a professional. And who knows how much longer I may not continue to do so?